Dark Times in Frankfort

William Schuster

II

Contents

Introduction...... V

~ Chapters ~

IV

Introduction

In researching the history of Frankfort for my first book, **Stories Forgotten Frankfort, N.Y.,** I uncovered the fact that after the community was incorporated in 1863, more than a dozen of its citizens had met their demise through foul play during the one hundred years following incorporation. Some of these murder cases have never been solved. Looking at the time periods during which multiple serious crimes occurred in the past, its obvious that homicides happened regularly in the first half of the last century. But after two murders in 1964, the village has been free of a capital offense for five decades, a record for its history. In each of the last three murder cases, committed during the 1960s, the victim was a woman. The opening chapter is very graphic and may be too explicit for some readers. Descriptive writing published in the past was very detailed when compared to news reporting in today's world. Frankfort gained notoriety when the murderer described in chapter eleven became the first American citizen to be extradited back to the United States. No person who had migrated from Italy and become a naturalized American citizen, then returned to Italy, had ever been given up by the Italian government to be taken back to the United States to face criminal charges. In the following pages I have covered four cases from the 19th century and thirteen that occurred during the twentieth century. Times have changed and perhaps no one will need to document such crimes in Frankfort during this century.

VI

Chapter 1

The Bigamist 1871

Families were large around the time of the American Civil War. Those were times when many young lives were taken by diseases no longer a threat today. Having several children provided the family with wage earners who could care for aging parents. Nancy Roland's six brothers and four sisters were mostly scattered around or in Frankfort. Nancy was a member of the Frankfort Methodist Episcopal Church on Main Street and was married to Lucian M. Sprague there. The marriage produced five children; first, two boys and then three girls. Lucian was taken by the Army, leaving Nancy to raise the five youngsters. It was during this time that friends described her as having a nervous temperament and being of delicate health. And then the worst news possible was received. Nancy's husband had died in the Army. She was now "widow Sprague" before reaching her fortieth birthday. The village was small but large enough to now be incorporated. It was home to the sprawling Gates Match

Factory. John Thomas, one of the village's more prosperous residents, invited the two older children, (boys soon to become teenagers) into his home where he would provide for them. Nancy gladly accepted the proposal and it turned out to be a good decision on her part. Harvey and George Sprague both turned out to be model citizens. In fact, Harvey became commissioner of highways, tax collector and was an active volunteer fireman in the village. His rich bass voice could be heard in the M.E. Church choir.

Nancy took over the responsibility of raising the three younger siblings, Mary, Allie and Ettie. The girls were all under the age of ten. But the shock of her sudden responsibility was dampened by receipt of a two thousand dollar government insurance payout from Lucian's U.S. Army insurance policy. The amount was substantial; the equivalent of over thirty-five thousand dollars today. With those funds, the young widow was able to purchase a small home on three acres of land in the "reservation" near the Erie Canal dry dock and within walking distance of a schoolhouse where the girls could attend classes. Nancy could also provide the necessities of life quite well for her small family. Friends figured she still had about a thousand dollars in reserve after purchasing the property. As this became well known in the community, several eligible young gentleman took notice. But for whatever reason, a man twenty years beyond Nancy's age was able to gain her attention. The relationship led to her marriage on September 8, 1870 to Dyer Pangburn, a man from the Town of Columbia. Pangburn moved into Nancy's house, becoming a stepfather to the three girls. She counted on him to help support the family, for he had a reputation in the community of being an industrious and sober worker. But, within weeks, her new husband's actions belied any esteem granted him by his neighbors. Not only did he fail to provide any support for his new family, but he became verbally abusive to his wife and stepchildren. He demanded that Nancy sign the property over to him or in any case, sell the property and split the proceeds. Nancy would have none of that and by December, only three months into the marriage, she clearly realized what Dyer's intentions were.

Nancy told Pangburn to move out of her property and informed him of her intention to obtain a divorce. He found work in the Town of Columbia and did leave Frankfort. Within weeks, however, he attempted to move back in, saying he had nowhere to stay. On several evenings he returned to the house and was refused entrance. In another attempt to enter the house he was greeted with a pan of scalding water. That incident led to his bringing a suit for assault against Nancy. Even after the assault, he continued to return to the property, again saying he had nowhere to go and in a moment of weakness, Nancy agreed that he could temporarily stay in the home, although no formal agreement was ever set. The relationship carried on in this manner through the winter and into the summer of 1871. When anything of value was purchased by either party the term "ours" was never used. Everything was "mine" or "yours" and living in the same household only led to an increasing deterioration of the relationship.

Eventually, the truth came out about Dyer Pangburn. He had served a sentence in Auburn prison after being convicted of bigamy. By one account, previous to his marriage to Nancy he had lived with four different women to whom he claimed to have been married. His previous neighbors considered him a Mormon in principle and practice. Children of his other marriages were scattered in areas near the Town of Columbia. Seven years after his marriage to Nancy took place, the United States Supreme Court upheld Congress' power to prohibit polygamy and set punishment for a married person marrying another at $500 and imprisonment of not more than five years. They ruled on a case brought by a member of the Mormon Church who declared that he was allowed to marry multiple women by his religious belief. The court concluded that people cannot excuse themselves from the law because of their religion and in 1890 the Church of Jesus Christ of Latter Day Saints issued a statement dissolving any marriages "forbidden by the law of the land." Dyer's demand that Nancy deed the property to him continued and her refusals only made him more abusive. It was now the middle of August in 1871, almost a year into the terrible union and Nancy continued her attempt to remove her gray-haired husband from the homestead and out of the lives of her daughters.

On Monday evening, August 14, 1871 Nancy was not feeling well. She had visited Dr. Skiff in the village earlier, and he had prescribed medication for her nervous condition. It was later revealed by the doctor that she had expressed her fear that Dyer would do her harm if she was unable to make him leave the property. While there was no arguing that day, Sunday had been another time of confrontation concerning his failure to move out of the house. Before sunset Nancy told

Dyer that she was not feeling well and would be sleeping downstairs with the girls. She asked him to sleep upstairs and he promptly refused. When the lamp was put out, he put a pillow on the floor behind a door of the parlor and slept there in view of Nancy and the girls.

What happened that night is taken from the testimony of ten-year-old Mary, a witness to a horrific crime. Just before midnight the children were awakened by screams coming from the adjoining kitchen. One of the younger girls was first to see what was happening and grabbed on to her older sister Mary shouting "Dyer is killing Ma." The three little girls went to the kitchen door and witnessed what no child should ever be subjected to. Dyer was standing over their mother with a large wooden potato masher. They saw him swing the club twice into her skull as she screamed "murder, murder!" The fiend yelled to the little ones to return to their beds or the same would happen to them. Fearing for their lives they ran back to the sleeping area where they continued to hear five or six more blows to their mother's head. That wooden potato masher was made of hardwood, fifteen inches long and three inches in diameter at the large end. Large enough and heavy enough to break Nancy's facial bones and skull. Nancy died before the process was over. The wooden tool had broken her skull open and her brain oozed out like jelly. The kitchen walls were splattered with blood and her lifeless body lie in a pool of blood. The children dared not move from the parlor, but heard the back door to the kitchen open and close several times before everything became silent. The terrified little ones were motionless and sleepless waiting for dawn. With the first light of day, the children dared to exit the parlor through a window and ran to Mr. Henry Walby's home, where they cried out their story. Soon the scene of the tragedy was swarming with neighbors. Friends of Nancy were in disbelief and warned by those who had gone into the kitchen not to enter the scene of the crime. A close neighbor, Mrs. Folts, claimed she had heard someone during the night and now presumed it was the murderer. A large group of men began a search for Dyer Pangburn and it was said that if found, the county would have little expense in the matter. The search party saw no problem with a vigilante type hanging of such a despicable character.

But that idea soon became unnecessary when Newton Stansel was heard shouting from the barn behind Nancy's home, announcing that he had found the murderer's lifeless stiff body hanging from a beam from a crudely fashioned rope noose. The rigid condition of the body gave a clue that Dyer had chosen to end his life shortly after the murder of his wife was completed. The beam was only about six feet above the ground but the position of the body gave evidence that the murderer was unwavering in his determination to leave a world he dared not face. An inquest was held in Frankfort with a five person jury led by Dr. Skiff and the conclusion was obvious.

In the case of Dyer Pangburn's death, the jury brought in a verdict that Mr. Pangburn did voluntarily, of his own malice and forethought hang and kill himself. In the case of the death of Nancy Sprague Pangburn, it was ruled that Dyer Pangburn of Frankfort made an assault with malice and forethought upon the body of his wife, inflicting mortal wounds upon her head that undoubtedly caused her death.

The three orphaned sisters were raised into adulthood by sympathetic members of the community and went on to full useful lives, but must have carried the scars of that terrible evening with them to the end.

Chapter 2

Me No Modoc 1875

I n 1873, citizens of the United States were outraged that Civil War hero General Edward Canby had been killed by a band of Modoc Indians near the California-Oregon border. The event led to the Modoc War, a small but deadly skirmish that took the lives of eighty-three whites and seventeen Modocs. Newspapers of the day sensationalized the short-lived war and soon the name Modoc was being disparaged by many Americans. That included a group of young men in Frankfort who spent their summer evenings "hanging out" at Graves' corner; Litchfield and Main Streets. The war occurred only a decade after the village had been chartered and those loitering on the corner were almost entirely of Anglo-Saxon heritage. They worried that their English-speaking community had been infiltrated by a group of darker skinned southern Europeans brought to Frankfort by companies seeking cheap labor for the railroads and Erie Canal. Frankfort's gang soon associated the name Modocs with these new, Italian-speaking, residents.

Italian men were brought to Frankfort by "padrones", English-speaking Italian contractors hired by the New York Central and Hudson River Railroad or the Erie Canal Authority. A Mr. Houghton had constructed cheap hemlock shanties near the Erie Canal towpath and rented them to the newcomers. The area is now known as Canal Street. This was the first period to see Italian immigrants in the village and was a decade before the West Shore Shops construction project brought a larger group of foreigners to town. Frankfort's largest industry at the time, the Gates Match factory, hired mostly women and children. The Italians, in spite of their slight builds and low stature were hired for vigorous manual labor.

Nineteen-year-old Jerillo Siegrelle was living in one of the towpath shanties with his father and brother. The family had been in Frankfort just over two years by June of 1875. The father spoke only Italian; the boys knew enough English to communicate with village merchants. Landlord Houghton considered the Siegrelles very stable and hard-working. They had paid their rent on time during the winter of 1874-75 when jobs were scarce and they attended strictly to their own affairs without problems, doing all of their own cooking in the room they shared with eight other immigrants. On the evening of June 3rd, young Jerillo (called Joe by everyone) had returned from his job as a laborer in Mohawk and was sent to the grocery by his father to purchase lard and potatoes. Besides bread, potatoes cooked in lard was a staple of the immigrant diet. Joe walked to Frankfort's main corner at Litchfield and Main streets where Crosby's store was located. He could not avoid the eyes of Frankfort's group of young men and had to pass in front of them to enter the store. As in previous encounters, expressions of low opinion were hurled at Joe by the loiterers. Joe entered the store and placed his order, but before his order was wrapped, he returned to the street and confronted the gang that had little to do except hang out on Graves' corner after stops at the Moran House bar, Crosby's Saloon or Billing's Saloon.

Immediately, Joe was the target of words meant to hurt. Similar remarks made earlier apparently were enough to cause him to return to the street before his order was complete. Within minutes, an event occurred that captured the emotions of the village and led to a further division between the natives and an increasing population of immigrants. "The Italian", as every witness later described Joe, produced a knife and stabbed twenty-two-year-old Michael Loftus. The victim was from a prominent Frankfort family and worked at the Armory in Ilion. He had two brothers and five sisters. Unfortunately, it was later revealed that Loftus and a nineteen-year-old friend named Lawrence Brown had only joined the group a few minutes before the stabbing occurred; they were regarded as better citizens than the rest of the group.

Joe possessed a small knife and plunged it toward Loftus a total of four times. The instrument penetrated Michael's body only twice, but the area of the punctures was critical, once over the heart and another under the heart. The upper wound severed a nerve connecting with the left arm, causing the arm to hang limp and lifeless. The other blow penetrated the left lung. Two arteries were severed and the flow of blood was stopped by keeping a finger pressed upon the upper wound. Michael Loftus cried out "good God, I'm stabbed" and later, while he was being assisted to Dr. Parkhurst's office a block away, he said he was dying. Lawrence Brown, the 19-year-old who accompanied Loftus when they had joined the group shortly before the stabbing, held his companion upright as they hurried to the doctor's office. Brown stated later that as they approached the engine house, halfway to the doctor's office, his wounded friend again said he knew he would die and at that moment Loftus lost consciousness as Brown heard a rattling and gurgling sound coming from Michael's throat. As they reached the sidewalk to Dr. Parkhurst's home, just beyond the Moyer Creek bridge, Michael slumped to the ground and had to be carried into the office.

The flow of blood was stopped by Dr. Parkhurst, but little could be done internally in those days to repair damage to vital organs and the doctor gave no hope that Michael could recover. On Friday, Michael Loftus died in the home of his parents, surrounded by his friends. On Monday, Coroner Robinson began an inquest into the case, which now became a murder. A jury was quickly impaneled, led by Dr. P.A. Skiff as foreman. The jury met at the Loftus residence and viewed the body, then went to the office of Attorney Joseph J. Duddleston Jr. where they questioned each member of the group that witnessed the crime.

Members of the Graves' corner group consisted of Roselle Smith, Robert Wilson, Eugene Widrick, John Dowd Jr., Ezra Louis and Lawrence Brown. While there were variations in each member's recall of the event, the story that emerged would lead one to believe that the confrontation with Joe Siegrelle would indeed end in the manner it did. The gang's actions that night were undoubtedly not the first time that an immigrant was fair sport and gave them entertainment. The verbal assault on Siegrelle conformed with feelings they had about the shanty people who spoke in a foreign tongue and looked different from the typical English-speaking American.

The epithets thrown out at Joe Siegrelle on that evening before he entered Crosby's grocery burned inside his psyche, forcing him to leave his purchases and confront the gang. The intimidation he encountered was readily admitted when each member of the gang was questioned by members of the jury. From testimony it was learned that when Joe crossed Litchfield Street someone yelled out "Here comes a Modoc." As Joe passed Robert Wilson he stopped after Wilson again called out "Modoc" and Joe asked Wilson why he called him that bad name, saying "Me no Modoc, me Italian, me cut your face." John Dowd Jr. responded by calling Joe a "buzzee." The gang had also been using that term to label the Italian immigrants as criminals. In 1838, Charles Dickens described Buz-Napper's Academy, a school that trained young thieves. Graduates became "buzzers" or, pickpockets. The gang was using both terms to insult Italian immigrants.

Testimony confirmed that Joe entered Crosby's grocery after the insults were shouted out to him, placing his order for potatoes and lard with clerk Chauncey Harter, but the verbal assault was too much for Joe to handle. He left without his order and confronted the group, only to receive another round of insults. Michael Loftus was closest to Joe and

Siegrelle called out to him "You bad man." Loftus said "No, you bad man."and the lone immigrant again replied "No, me no bad man, you bad man." At this point, the stabbing of Loftus occurred and Siegrelle ran toward Orchard Street, pursued by Smith and Wilson. At the dyke, the pursuers were turned back when Joe once again drew his knife and lunged at them. When they backed off on their pursuit, the assailant continued on a path away from the village.

Deputy Sheriff Thomas Honohan started a search as soon as he was informed of the stabbing. His immediate response was to visit the shanties along the canal towpath, bringing with him two witnesses from the gang. At the time, the extent of Loftus' injuries were unknown to both the assailant and his pursuers. Honohan and the witnesses were allowed to inspect the room that housed eleven men including the Siegrelles. By the light of a lantern they saw a man sleeping that resembled the assailant, but the two witnesses failed to identify him as Joe Siegrelle and no one was arrested. The deputy sheriff left the Houghton shanties without a suspect, but later it would be learned that it was indeed Joe, pretending to be asleep during the search. It was also learned later that after the deputy sheriff left, Joe went to the neighborhood near Dr. Parkhurst's office and inquired about the extent of Michael Loftus' injuries. When he learned that the man he had stabbed would probably not live, Joe immediately left town.

The next morning Sheriff Honohan organized a large group of citizens to search for the assailant. A tip was received from a man who had been fishing the Mohawk River at 4a.m. He claimed to have seen three men walking from the village headed toward Utica when a man came out of the woods on the large hill along the road and met them. He claimed that he saw these men give objects to the lone man. Sheriff Honohan surmised that a change of clothing was probably provided the escapee and he directed a search, near the driving park, east of Utica, where another report was received that a party of fishermen there had provided a short man fitting Siegrelle's description with food. They described him as wearing black clothing. In Frankfort, Joe was wearing brown clothing.

After Loftus died, the excitement in Frankfort was intense. Threats were made to burn the shanties where the immigrants lived and to stone the "Italians" out of the village. But it didn't come to that after two more search parties were organized, armed with knives, pistols and guns. For a full week searchers sought the escapee in East Utica and even in the Town of Deerfield, turning up nothing. On June 10th the state added five hundred dollars to the Herkimer County Sheriff's previous five hundred dollar reward for Siegrelle's capture. On June 16th, a reported sighting of the fugitive at Clayville sent the armed search party there without success. Before that, on June 14th, it was learned that Joe's father and brother had left Frankfort. No record could be found that Jerrilo "Joe" Siegrelle was ever captured and arrested.

Several interesting facts were revealed during the inquest when Joe's brother James was questioned. He admitted that it was indeed Joe that was in bed and not identified during the sheriff's search of the shanty. And he verified that Joe had gone to Dr. Parkhurst's home to inquire about the extent of the injuries that he had inflicted. He claimed that Joe had over one hundred fifty dollars on his person when he fled. That would be over three thousand dollars today. But the most disturbing statement his brother made was that "Joe, he had trouble in the head."

Less than two years later, two of the witnesses called upon to testify at the inquest, Roselle Smith and Eugene Widrick were convicted of arson in the burning of the Winant Hotel, at the corner opposite Crosby's store. The chapter "A Gang of Thieves & Fire Bugs" in my book Stories Forgotten Frankfort, NY tells that story. Widrick was pardoned by the governor after he testified for the state. Roselle Smith was sentenced to seven years in Auburn prison but died in his first year of incarceration at the age of twenty-eight.

Sharp criticism was put forth by the **Utica Morning Herald Newspaper** after they printed the story of the stabbing. It gave Frankfort residents a piece of advice about future dealings with the immigrant community:

A Lesson
It is to be hoped that this lamentable occurrence will teach a lesson to the young men of Frankfort. In this case, as is usual, an innocent man is the victim. But those who have made a game of the Italians for some time past, and abused them, considered it a legitimate sport, and were, perhaps, lead on by those who tacitly approved their course. As long as the Italians offended no one, and attended to their own affairs, they should have been unmolested.

Less than a decade later, before construction of the West Shore shops at Frankfort had begun, the **Utica Morning Herald and Daily Gazette** published a story about conditions the Italian immigrants had to endure after they arrived here as laborers in the construction of the railroads. The story is as it was published:

The majority of the laborers employed are from Italy. The Italians are light limbed and thin blooded who cannot mind an hour of cold weather. They are employed in squads of fifty or one hundred thru Signor Brazelle of the Italian Union in New York City. The union is an organization after the style of the Chinese companies of San Francisco. It imports thousands of Italians to fill contracts, advances money to pay their passage across the water and railroad fares. It sends out a corps of laborers in the charge of foremen who speak the English language. Each laborer wears a number around his neck known by the time-keeper and paymaster. They are housed in plain hemlock shanties with open windows only in the lower part. Within there are hung board tables, like those used on picnic grounds. On all sides of the rooms are bunks placed closely together in tiers that crowd the ceilings closely. Bunks are placed in the dark attic, every inch of floor is utilized for sleeping purposes. The Italians carry all of their clothing upon their persons and their daily stipend of bread in a canvas bag. They sleep in their clothing from one week to another. I have never found one with soap and towel thus far. Their daily food is dried bread, with water at each meal and occasionally coarse, cheap macaroni. Occasionally they buy lard with which they fry potatoes and soak into their bread. One of the foreman ordered five barrels of cider to the shanty while I was there. This he will retail to the men at a handsome profit. The men carry their money in belts about their persons and each man has a keen sharp knife or stiletto which he will use upon brief provocation. As a rule they are not quarrelsome, but are quick and treacherous, especially when intoxicated. Many send their money home to Italy. They crowd around the fires after supper and get as warm as possible and then they crowd into the shanties to sleep. A shanty twenty feet square will accommodate one hundred laborers, the more the merrier, as a crowded sleeping room is always warm. They do not mind the vile odors which are exhaled from the long-worn clothing and unwashed bodies – odors that would stifle an American citizen if he approached within two feet of the door of the shanty. The Italians mind their own business, and seldom, if ever, visit the neighboring villages. The one dollar daily wage will be advanced up to one dollar and fifty cents as they make themselves useful. The supply of Italians is unlimited.

Chapter 3

Who Killed the Old German? 1884

Before tracks were laid through the village by the New York, West Shore and Buffalo Railroad Company and the huge complex of repair shops was built, Frankfort's railroad depot was located at the New York Central's main line, north of the Mohawk River. It was a long walk from Main Street to the depot and a horse drawn service was available to transport passengers to and from the station. The land around the depot was developed into several plots where houses were built; homes for Frankfort natives who were then actually living in the Town of Schuyler. Once the repair shops were built in the village, the Central's depot was closed and the village's railroad station was opened just north of Orchard Street. In 1884, one of the houses between the New York Central tracks and the Schuyler to Herkimer Road was occupied by the Wishart family. It was the year that the West Shore shops opened in the village. John Wishart and his brother had come from Germany when John was thirty-one years old. He was now seventy. When he came to Frankfort, the Gates Match Company had started a rapid expansion and hiring spree and there were many other businesses where jobs could be found along the path of the Erie Canal or on the farms that now encompassed the small village.

John had married Nancy Widrick in Stone Arabia, a tiny community near Fort Plain. He was a sober man but had few skills and was limited to obtaining only manual labor positions to support his family. During his prime years, large groups of European laborers were brought to the Mohawk Valley for railroad and canal work, often working at lower wages than natives had been earning. John had bitter feelings toward the immigrants that he thought were affecting his ability to put food on the table as his family grew. And grow it did; almost yearly, to a point where John and Nancy had twelve children. He was disturbed that the "padrones" were bringing in so many Italian laborers to the village and was personally affected when two of his daughters were courted by Italians. By the time John was in his sixties he was only able to find work on farms in proximity to his home. Farmers were still in the process of clearing land and turning it into pasture in those days and John hired out to clear witch hazel on the flats adjacent to the Mohawk River, a demanding job for a man approaching seventy.

The Wishart children were brought up in terrible poverty and lacked any discipline demanding they be educated. Many could not read and write. Their priority seemed to be marrying young and moving out of the Wishart home. Mary, the oldest daughter, married Ilion carpenter Carlton Johnson. Annette married a Schuyler farmer named George Maxwell. Barbara, first living with two Italian laborers and after one of them was murdered, became Barbara Van Brocklin and moved to Adams, New York. Kathleen and Julia drew their fathers ire by marrying Italian immigrants. Kathleen, however, married Joseph Frank, a man who had lived in Frankfort for ten years, highly respected by villagers and said to have not associated with those considered in a lower class of the new immigrants. Julia was another case, having chased and married Italian workers on the West Shore rail line near the west side of the Hudson River Valley. That was where she met Michael Coach, an English speaking crew leader who had been in the country longer than most of his gang of railroad laborers. The family's youngest daughter, Louisa, had just become a teenager after Julia married Michael Coach and Coach began bringing a few of the Italian laborers he supervised on the railroad to the Wishart home.

Before Barbara married, she became involved with other Italian railroad workers in the area. The Utica, Susquehanna and Chenango Valley Railroad Company was engaged in laying track from Utica to Cassville and Waterville in the 1870s. Barbara left the Wishart home to live with one of those workers and she may have been the reason an Italian worker was shot and killed by a fellow countryman. The railroad company owned a large boarding house on Babcock Hill Road, one mile south of Cassville. Four families comprised of ten men, four women and three children were living there and Barbara Wishart was one of the women living in the house with an immigrant worker.

Barbara was living with Joseph Chion when newcomer Michael Rock came from New York City and was hired as a laborer. The story told at the time was that both men became infatuated with Barbara. Only one week after his arrival, Rock, along with most of the men in the house began drinking at a party on the front lawn. Joseph Chion and his mistress Barbara were inside the house. Evidently, the two men seeking the same woman had had a conversation in Italian previously; an exchange that became heated, and Rock left the house. This was a dangerous situation as each man carried a revolver and sure enough, Rock, finding a broken window, fired two shots into the house. One bullet found its target. Chion was hit in the eye, the bullet passing out of the back of his head, killing him instantly. Rock escaped and was pursued by members of a posse that consisted of a total of two hundred men. At an inquest held the following day, Barbara Wishart amazed everyone by testifying that the shooting by thirty-year-old Rock was in self defense. Chion was forty and in the end, Barbara defended the younger man. As Rock was being sought, the sheriff arrested Barbara, after a Polish immigrant who had been living in the house with the Italians, came forward and testified that Chion had never made an attempt to defend himself by retrieving his pistol lying on the stove. Barbara Wishart was released and returned to Frankfort several weeks later when it was assumed that Michael Rock had successfully fled to Italy.

Of six sons, George was the oldest and used his mother's maiden surname, Widrick. George Widrick was employed by the New York Central Railroad and moved to Syracuse. Charles, William, Fred, Alonzo and Adam lived in the area. By age seventy, John Wishart, still called "the German" and now referred to as the "old man", the father of twelve children found himself embroiled in controversy over providing for his wife, his youngest child and family members who would move back home from time to time. According to neighbors, outbursts of screaming and crying now became a regular occurrence around the Wishart home. John's only source of income was that coming from manual labor he performed at nearby farms and he had told his employers that he was being treated badly at home by both his wife and some of his children. He claimed that during times when he was able to bring money home, he was treated decently, but as his money disappeared, he was told to "get out". He confided in one farmer, telling him that he was saving a cache of money that he carried on his person with the intention of using it to return to Germany.

In January 1884, another Italian came into John's life. His Italian son-in-law, Michael Coach, then living in John's house with his wife Julia, brought a man known as Frank Wendon to the house. Frank was a thirty year old member of Coach's work crew and was a man he knew in Italy. Frank asked if he could board at the Wishart home, for he desired to get away from the terrible conditions at the shanty near the Erie Canal towpath where dozens of immigrants were crowded into one room. John was adamant that Frank not move in, showing his disdain for Italians, but his wife Nancy approved, just as she had approved the marriages of Julia and Kate to Italians. Nancy threatened John with removal from the residence if he did not agree to let Frank board in their home and in short time, Frank Wendon moved in. Frank's presence angered John to the point where he began leaving the house for days at a time, staying with his oldest son, George, now living in Syracuse, one of his daughters or even one of the farmers nearby. He would return home with a small amount of money and would be treated decently, as long as the money lasted. When abusive conditions prevailed again he would repeat the pattern and move out of the house.

As spring arrived, John was able to find work and he began adding to his secret cache of money for his return to Germany. Sanford Getman, his employer, and another man hired to help clear Getman's property, were probably the only people who knew about John's savings. The man helping him was a Hungarian who had settled with that ethnic group near Little Falls. He was known only as "the Hungarian" and he rented a room in Frankfort. John had many conversations with Sanford Getman about things happening in his life since "the Italian", Frank Wendon, moved into his house. He complained about a group of Italian laborers "hanging out" at his home now that both his son-in-law, Michael Coach and Frank were at the house. In addition to his family driving him out when the money was gone, he claimed that frequent rowdy parties were being held at his house, complete with alcohol and music. Getman advised John not to return to the house. John disagreed and once again claimed he would be returning to Germany.

John was back home when one of the dances was being held, complete with accordion and bagpipe music. A chair was broken and John started removing chairs from the house claiming they were his chairs. His wife Nancy taunted him by sitting on the lap of one of the Italian immigrants and his own sons and daughters physically removed him from the house. At that point it was said that Frank Wendon, the boarder, made a threat that he would throw John from the nearby Mohawk River bridge. John returned to Getman's place and during his stay revealed an amazing fact. Frank Wendon and John's daughter Louisa had been married by the Methodist minister in Frankfort. John had protested but Nancy had given her approval. Many were shocked by the announcement; Wendon was thirty years old and Louisa was thirteen!

In April, warmer weather meant more work for John at the Getman farm. He and the Hungarian worked together daily, clearing witch hazel brush on the meadows near the river, providing more pasture for the Getman farm. But during the third week of April, both John and the Hungarian were nowhere to be found. The Hungarian had been living in the village and his landlord reported that he had skipped out on his board bill. The last sighting of John was by his son, Adam, around April fifteenth and after that date, both workers failed to show up at the Getman farm. Everyone including his wife, Nancy, surmised that the old man probably went to Syracuse or Utica, staying with a son or daughter. But almost three weeks passed by and after contacting the out-of-town children and being told their father had not been there, it was agreed to begin a search of the area near Getman's farm. It was suggested that a creek running into the Mohawk River be searched.

Adam, the son that last saw his father, discovered a body in the creek on May eighth. It was John Wishart and his head had an obvious injury. Adam was the last one to see his father and was also the one that found his father's body. The district attorney later pointed this fact out when questioning Adam about his involvement. The news spread through the Village of Frankfort causing a state of excitement on the streets. Officials announced that an inquest would be held on the following day in Loftis Hall on Main Street. The body was taken to the village and Frankfort's three prominent doctors, W.W. Budlong, W.H.H. Parkhurst and G.N. Lehr performed a post mortem examination. Their ruling was both unanimous and obvious. John Wishart's death had been caused by blows to his head made by someone wielding a blunt object, but not made of metal; a metal instrument would have penetrated and deeply cut the scalp. A heavy club-like wooden stick, two inches thick, was found near the body. It was in a broken condition and had a tuft of John's hair clinging to it. A depression over the skull fracture matched the knob-end of the club and it was deemed to be the murder weapon. After questioning John's son Adam and the property owner, Sanford Getman, police officials began a search for the missing Hungarian, the only other man that was working near the location where the body was found. Since he had left his room in the village, police went to a colony near Little Falls and interviewed Hungarian immigrants. No one had seen him. In many minds, the missing man was the prime suspect and the probable murderer of John Wishart.

If John had disclosed the fact that he was carrying a considerable amount of money on his person for his return trip to Germany, the Hungarian who had disappeared would indeed be a prime suspect. But as detectives interviewed neighbors and family members, another path was uncovered that led them back to those living in John Wishart's home. The personal information provided to Sanford Getman by John about his treatment by both family members and his new son-in-law, Frank Wendon, threw suspicion upon the entire group. Authorities had liberal powers of investigation during that time period and were able to react quickly. Before the inquest had begun on the day following the murder, John's wife, Nancy (called old lady Wishart in newspapers), the Italian immigrant Frank Wendon, his child bride Louisa and the Wishart's son Fred, along with his wife, were placed under arrest and brought before Judge Ingham.

During her arraignment, young Louisa made a statement which may have immediately incriminated the group. She said it was foolish to make so much fuss over an old fool like her father. But all proclaimed their innocence in the matter and the women wept copiously. Frank Wendon was placed in the village lockup and the four other family members taken to adjoining rooms in the Central Hotel at the corner of Main Street and Litchfield Street. Officer Finster stood guard in the hallway. After the first day of the inquest was held at Loftis Hall, all five detainees were taken to the Herkimer County Jail.

Testimony was taken at the inquest and details were revealed about occurrences at the Wishart household prior to the murder. Quickly, suspicions turned away from the missing Hungarian and fingers started pointing to the family itself, especially the new Italian son-in-law. Michael Coach, the Italian work crew leader and husband of Wishart's daughter Julia, held nothing back in his testimony about the Italian immigrant, Frank Wendon, the man he brought to the Wishart home, now the husband of John's teenage daughter Louisa. When Coach was questioned about his friend Wendon, the first discrepancy discovered was a mistake made by both police officials and the press in the proper spelling of the man's name. Coach stated that the man he had brought to the Wishart home in the fall of 1883 was Francisca Mundone, not Frank Wendon. He was a married man who spent eight months in a jail in Poteuza, Italy, a small town in Calabria. He had been convicted of an assault on a "very young girl." The revelation caused a roar in the crowd of over one hundred in Loftis Hall as they knew that this man had now married a thirteen-year-old daughter of the victim.

Previous testimony by the officers who had arrested and taken the family members to the village for detainment had already caused whispers amongst those in attendance at the hearing when it was revealed that they had found Frank and his child bride Louisa in bed, completely nude at the time of their arrest. The daily hearings featured testimony by family members who claimed to have heard Mundone threaten John Wishart with bodily harm after Mundone had moved into the Wishart home and later married Louisa.

Hearings were held daily during the two weeks following the discovery of John Wishart's body and the possibility that the missing Hungarian committed the crime vanished. All fingers were pointing toward the new son-in-law, Francisca Mundone as the one who had a motive. Did he act alone or did Mrs. Wishart and other family members have a part in the act? That was the question that had to be answered. The case attracted statewide attention because if Mundone was convicted of premeditated murder, he would be the first person to be sentenced to hang at the Herkimer County Jail. Loftis Hall was packed and reporters from across the state eagerly wired their stories to home offices. If Mundone was proven guilty, those reporters would exploit the fact that he was another "Italian" murderer in Frankfort like Jerillo Siegrelle nine years previous; an "Italian" who escaped prosecution. There was still a vocal group of villagers talking about tearing down the immigrant shanties along the Erie Canal and driving "the Italians" from town. Reporters of the day wasted no time in demeaning the Italian immigrants. One of the first reports about the inquest described the Wishart home as a small and poorly furnished house that "has lately been the resort and lounging place of Italians and persons of doubtful character." Sanford Getman, owner of the property where John Wishart had been working, was named foreman of the seven man inquest panel but also provided the most information about Mundone's possible motive for the crime.

Getman revealed that the murder victim talked to him many times about personal family matters. Wishart had told him almost a year previous to his disappearance that his wife Nancy had threatened to split his head open with an ax, made him sleep on the floor without proper clothing and sometimes kicked him outside. Wishart's son Adam, who found the body, testified that his new Italian brother-in-law, Mundone, had threatened to throw his father off the Mohawk River bridge some dark night. When Frank Mundone took the stand, the district attorney revealed the fact that Mundone came from Italy as a married man and when asked where his wife was, his reply was that she had taken another husband in Italy before he had married the victim's daughter Louisa. The broken stick believed to be the murder weapon was shown to Mundone and he was asked if he had struck John with it and in the process broke it into two pieces. Joseph

Frank, husband of Wishart's daughter Kate acted as an interpreter and gave Mundone's response:

"No I did not look where John went; I did not use and break the stick." "If I fix John with that, I would have gone back to Italy."

"I last saw John alive three weeks ago on the bridge near the house, walking with the Hungarian. I do not know the name of the Hungarian and I never saw the stick before. I would never do such a thing as strike John with that stick. I never said that if John did not leave me alone I would lick him and I never told John I would throw him off the bridge."

A reporter for the *Rome Daily Sentinel* gained access to interview Mrs. Nancy Wishart and her daughter Louisa while they were being held at the Central Hotel. The interview was frank and revealing:

"Louisa and I first saw Mundone when he came to our house to board last fall. He and Mike Coach, Julia's husband, were friends in Italy. Mike came to this country first and when the West Shore work started, he worked along the Hudson River at different points and in the Mohawk Valley. Julia went down east last summer with one of her Italian husbands and became acquainted with Coach. Then Mundone, who had come to this country some time before, went to work in a gang of men under Coach. Julia soon afterword came home and was soon followed here by Mundone. The old man at that time did not do anything to support the family. He abused the children and would have abused me if I had not been able to defend myself. Mundone supported us all and Julia would not allow the old man to live on him. That is the only reason why the old man did not like him. He did not care for the child. Last winter Mike coach talked of going to Italy, but Julia did not want him to go. She begged Mundone to influence Coach to

stay in America, but Mundone, then living with Julia, did not care to do so. Mundone had taken quite a notion to Louisa, who was a child, to be sure, but we prevented him from getting with her which probably made him like her still more. Julia finally thought it would be well to have Mundone get Coach to come to Frankfort and he (Mundone) marry Louisa. That pleased Mundone and they asked my consent, and I, thinking that she might get into some worse trouble, said yes."

"When did you see John Wishart last?" asked the reporter.

"He left the house about three weeks ago with a Hungarian and went down toward the depot. That is the last I saw of him. I had wondered where he had gone and asked Alonso if he had seen him and he said no."

"Do you think anyone of your family killed him?"

"No, I do not. We have all had our troubles and quarrels and have said many rough things. But after all, I do not think anyone in the family, either my children or son-in-law hated the old man enough to kill him."

"Who do you think killed him?"

"I don't know. He was in the habit of talking freely to anyone who would talk with him. He had said a great deal about saving money to go to Germany. I don't know how much he had saved. He earned money but did not spend it for the family, nor for drink. If he had money saved he would be likely to tell it to any stranger, but he would not tell his family. It may be that someone thought he had money about him and killed him to get it."

Mrs. Wishart denied the statement made to Sanford Getman by her husband that she had said she would split his head open with an ax.

"Are Coach and Mundone good friends now?"

"No, they are bitter enemies. Mundone received a letter from his first wife in Italy and in that letter was a half sheet for Coach, written by his father, wanting him to come to Italy and bring with him two or three hundred dollars. Mundone took the note to Coach

and read it. Coach then accused Mundone of opening his letters and reading them and they have been enemies ever since."

As the inquest at Loftis Hall progressed, many members of the family were called to testify. Alonzo Wishart took the stand and was described by reporters as a weak minded, ignorant fellow who certified to nothing important. He swore he did not know how old he was, or even what his mother's first name was. Adam Wishart's wife Hattie was described as the most serious and reliable witness, testifing that she had heard Frank Mundone threaten her father-in-law. The three physicians described in great detail the wounds that caused Wishart's death; all agreed that the broken wooden club displayed was the murder weapon.

John Wishart's son William, a farmhand, said he had not been near his father's home recently, and had not heard of any inquiries as to his father's whereabouts. He had heard that his youngest sister had married an Italian, a man he knew, having worked with him in Oneida. He and Mundone had worked on a project together laying water pipe one year earlier. But then his testimony became very important when he claimed to have heard Mundone make remarks about his father the last time he had visited his father's house. "I heard the Italian say that he would make away with my father sometime; he was not talking to me, as I was in another room and my father was not in the house at the time. I was in the kitchen and the Italian was in the sitting room; do not know who he was talking with. I know a few French words."

Frank Bridenbecker was another area farmer that had hired John Wishart to clear land along with the Hungarian.

He testified that John had come to work one morning and appeared very mad; he said his daughter Julia had told him that she heard the Italian say he would kill him. Like Sanford Getman, Bridenbecker said he advised John to get out of the house. He said John was emphatic that Mundone would not drive him from his home and then went on at length about the Italians hanging out there, remarking that he had seen the Italian, now his son-in-law with a pistol. He said he was going to the Frankfort police and have him arrested for carrying a concealed weapon. It was at this point during the coroner's inquest when attention turned to Frank Mundone as the murderer and away from the missing Hungarian.

The Wishart's son Fred's wife, Bessie George, was called to testify and the press was enthralled to have her on the stand. They described her as an apparently simpleminded girl of about sixteen years. She testified that the woman, Mrs. George, who was called her mother, was not her own mother. When she lived with Mrs. George she was not allowed to go to school or work out, but was compelled to go out in rags, begging in the neighborhood. She had been to school only four days in her life. She married Fred and they lived with the Wishart family. Her testimony touched the hearts of those present in Loftis Hall. She testified that Louisa, Mundone's child bride was very abusive to the old man and drove him out of the house on more than one occasion. She had seen Louisa hit the old man with a stick and said the old woman was also abusive to her husband. She was in the house when a quarrel took place between the old man, his wife and Frank Mundone. She then made the statement "I saw the old man leave the house, followed by Frank

Mundone who carried a large stick with him." At that point in her testimony the district attorney showed her the broken stick believed to be the weapon used to kill John Wishart and asked her if it was the stick carried by Mundone. She replied that it looked like the same club and added that the old man and Frank were still quarreling as they left the house. She remembered that the old man said he would have Frank arrested for having two wives. But undoubtedly the most important testimony of the entire several days of the inquest was her revelation that she witnessed what happened at the house when Frank Mundone came back home after he followed John Wishart with the stick that morning. Bessie claimed "Louisa, Frank and mother shut themselves up in a bedroom and were closed up in there for some time. When mother came out she looked like she had been crying."

Bessie George's testimony was followed by that of Mrs. George who testified that the "Italians" came to the Wishart home nightly and the "old man" did not like it. She claimed Nancy Wishart abused her husband and would scratch and choke him. The next day's testimony included John Lewis' description of quarreling he had heard coming from the Wishart house. He lived about forty rods (660') away and claimed he heard the old man cry out "Oh Nancy don't"and figured Mrs. Wishart was beating her husband. He said there were frequent bouts of loud shouting coming from the house, especially during the dances. Julia, the wife of Mike Coach, the man who brought Mundone to the Wishart home, also made a statement that Mundone had threatened the old man and later told her that if an old man like her father was in Italy that he would "chee" him. Supposedly, that word was interpreted by her to mean he would kill him.

Before testimony was wrapped up after six days of a seemingly endless parade of neighbors, family members and public officials taking the stand, the one hundred or more villagers packing Loftis Hall, along with newspaper reporters covering the story, were quite certain that Frank Mundone would be indicted for the murder. The question remaining to be answered concerned the part both Mrs. Wishart and daughter Louisa played in the event. To further build a case against Mundone, the district attorney described the murdered man's attempt to have Frankfort Police arrest Mundone for carrying a concealed weapon. James H. Watkins testified that Mr. Wishart came to him and described abuse he was suffering at home by both his family and Mundone. He wanted a warrant issued for both his son Fred and Mundone. The lawyer said he explained to Wishart that he would need to produce a witness to the events described.

The *Utica Sunday Tribune*'s headline summed up conclusions being made by the public:

A COLD-BLOODED FAMILY

By Monday, May nineteenth, at 5:15 p.m., all evidence was declared in and the jury retired. They were only out about one half hour and returned the following verdict:

That on the 17th day of April, 1884, at the Town of Schuyler in said county of Herkimer, one Frank Mundone did strike the said John Wishart with a club or other heavy instrument, which he then and there had and held in his hand and feloniously and with malice of aforethought, and with intent to kill him, the said John Wishart, and that the said Frank Mundone at the time and place aforesaid, willfully, feloniously and of malice of aforethought, the said John Wishart did kill and murder; and the jurors aforesaid, upon their oaths aforesaid, do further say that Nancy Wishart and Louisa Mundone, abetted, aided, counseled and assisted the said Frank Mundone in the commission of said offense and in the killing and murdering John Wishart at the time and in the manner above set forth.

The three prisoners were returned to the Herkimer County Jail for a stay that would last at least until a Grand Jury's final decision on indictment. As it turned out, this would be many months and in Frank Mundone's case, years.

If convicted of first degree murder, Frank Mundone would face the gallows and become Herkimer County's first hanging. But an appeal was filed by a Frankfort attorney and within six months, on November 18, 1884 the determination of the corner's inquest was affirmed by the court. By that date, Nancy Wishart and her daughter Louisa Mundone were released on bail after spending several months in jail. In January of 1885, another infamous murderer joined Frank in a nearby cell. Roxalana Druse was later convicted of killing and dismembering her husband near Richfield Springs. She did indeed become Herkimer County's first hanging, a botched hanging that would spur New York State to use the electric chair for future executions. The winter of 1884 to 1885 was long and cold; Frank sat in his cell awaiting the gathering of the grand jury. Finally, the proceedings were set in motion on May 18, 1885.

During the trial held from May 18th to May 22nd, many of the same witnesses heard at the corner's inquest testified and the same stories were repeated. But new testimony was given by County Sheriff Brown. Brown said that in June of 1884, during the first month of Mundone's confinement, the prisoner said he wished to see him in the dining room, as he wanted to tell him something. The sheriff took the prisoner to his office and they talked for almost two hours. Frank said he wanted to tell the real story about how John Wishart was killed.

Frank's story: "I stood on the Frankfort bridge waiting for a train on which I expected some friends. I saw Adam Wishart fishing from a boat in the river below. He crossed the river and I walked down to the railroad track. I then saw Adam come from the bushes along the bank of the river. Then I saw John Wishart, coming from a clump of witch hazel bushes and go down the tracks as far as Mr. Getman's crossing. This is the place that I saw Adam come out and make motions for his father to come to him. I then saw Adam hit old John over the head five or six times and in the face; he then pulled him into the bushes. That was the last time I ever saw John Wishart. After I saw the crime I stayed under a tree until nine or ten o'clock that night, afraid the Wishart boys would kill me."

Sheriff Brown took charge of the prisoner and took him to the crime scene where he repeated his story that Adam Wishart killed his father. But when he returned to Herkimer, the sheriff witnessed actions by Mundone that undermined his credibility. As the prisoners were going out in the yard, Frank ran to the cell occupied by his mother-in-law Nancy Wishart and said "Miss Wish, Miss Wish, you swear just the same as I do and we will get out in a little while". Later, with the district attorney present, Louisa Mundone, broken by her time spent in jail, finally turned on her husband and yelled out to him for all to hear, "You say my brother killed old John. You killed him yourself and you told me so yourself in the bedroom. You told me if I told my mother you would kill me. You told me two or three times that you killed old John and throwed him in the ditch." Frank then called his teen bride a liar and told Sheriff Brown a new version of the story. He now claimed that both he and Adam killed John Wishart and he went home and told Nancy Wishart that they had killed John. When she cried, Mundone said "What for you cry? You said you wanted him killed." A few more witnesses were heard in the last days of the trial and again it was repeated testimony, but Sheriff Brown's new information probably sealed the fate of Francisca Mundone.

The sudden disappearance of John Wishart's Hungarian work partner, skipping out on his board bill and not returning to the Hungarian colony at Little Falls, could now be explained simply as a matter of fear of being accused of the crime. If he discovered the body upon showing up to work with Wishart, running away may have been and probably was his first instinct.

The twelve-man jury was shown photographs, the broken club believed to be the murder weapon and the actual skull of the victim that had a fracture believed to have caused death. The verdict was as expected but differed from the ruling of the Frankfort inquest a year earlier. No indictment was declared for wife Nancy Wishart or her daughter Louisa Mundone this time. But Justice Williams affirmed the indictment of Frank Mudone for first degree murder; a ruling that included a sentence that he be hanged in the yard of the Herkimer County Jail on July 10th, only seven weeks away. Mundone's attorney from Frankfort, J.J. Dudleston, filed an appeal to the general term and it was taken. But the judicial ruling made on November 18th affirmed the conviction of first degree murder and it was again reported that a hanging would take place early in 1886. Once again an appeal was filed on that ruling and Mundone sat in jail until the appeal was heard in October of 1886. He had been in the Herkimer County Jail for two years and four months.

Just a few months before the Court of Appeals met again, Mundone's child bride Louisa, now fifteen years old, died at the Wishart home on August 25, 1886. Nine months earlier a reporter wrote: "So strongly attached is the family to the Italians, that for some time Louisa has been living with one of them as his wife, although not married, and it is reported and generally believed that Nancy Wishart, widow of the murdered German, is married to another of the sons of the same clime." The announcement of Louisa's death, printed in newspapers of the day, is a great example of the prejudice openly shown to those who had migrated from Italy and Sicily:

> Louisa, the child wife of Frank Mundone, the Italian murderer who is awaiting the execution of death sentence in the Herkimer jail, died yesterday at the Wishart residence. Ever since she was released from jail, where she was confined for several months, charged with the murder of her father, this unfortunate child has been living with or been the companion of Italians, and now yet in her teens, goes to her grave a victim of her own folly. For the past ten years, and long before the murder of John Wishart, a majority of the female members of the family seemed possessed by a desire to associate with Italians and many are the times they have appeared in police court to have grievances heard and settled. Nancy Wishart, the mother, and widow of the murdered German, soon after her husband's tragic death, was living in this village with an

Italian. For some months Louisa has been gradually failing in health, and has received such care as the family were able to bestow, aided by a physician a part of the time. Since her release from jail Louisa has manifested a stolid indifference with reference to her husband's fate. When asked concerning Frank and the fate awaiting him, she shouted an indifferent "I don't care." No undertaker has been called, the family themselves performing the services usually done by others. The funeral will occur from the Wishart residence Friday.

The appeal heard in October reversed the previous decisions of first degree murder and on October 12, 1886, almost two and one half years after Francisa Mundone was first confined to a jail cell, a new trial was ordered. Officials were livid; the Wishart murder trial had cost the municipalities thousands of dollars, probably the most expensive trial ever held in Herkimer County. One hundred and fifty jurors from all parts of the county were called up for a trial to be started in December. This was at the same time that the trial of Roxalana Druse was being held. Herkimer County Court was about to be very busy.

But a jury was not required! Francisa Mundone accepted a plea of guilty to second degree murder on December 4, 1886; the one hundred and fifty jurors gathered at the courthouse at 9a.m. were released and the tax payers relieved of the expense of another trial. Newspaper headlines shouted "Ended at Last!" Judge Williams accepted the plea and sentenced Mundone to hard labor at Auburn State Prison for the rest of his life. The judge gave a lengthy and almost tedious explanation to the court of his justification for accepting the plea.

Francisa Mundone was allowed to address the judge and held nothing back. He said he had been held in jail three years because he had been lied about and said it was because he was an Italian man.

Chapter 4

Trouble in the Railyard 1884

Spring came right on schedule in the year 1885. The Village of Frankfort was booming. New homes, retail shops and even new hotels were being built. The hard work of raising seventy-seven thousand dollars to bring the West Shore Railroad repair shops into town accomplished its goal and a huge complex of buildings was constructed during the previous two years, lining the north side of East Main Street. The miles of rail required to direct cars and engines to the proper repair shop was still a work in progress. A huge circular roundhouse, utilized for minor repairs, avoided moving the big engines into the main erecting shop (the large building that later became Union Fork and Hoe Company's forge shop), where major rebuilding was accomplished. When the weather broke in April, a yard crew under the supervision of Joseph Rouso was assigned the job of installing connecting rails to the roundhouse. Crews were grouped by ethnicity due to language barriers. He directed German, Swedish, Polish and Italian laborers in different areas of the railyard.

Most of the German and Swedish workers had been employed by the railroad company for the previous two year construction period and appeared to be satisfied with their laborer jobs, glad to have a job in their new country. The Italian and Polish immigrants were handicapped by the language difficulties they encountered and each was assigned an identification number stamped on a metal tag which hung from their necks. They too were glad to have a job in their new country and took any assignment readily. Few problems between the different work crews were noted as long as they were separated in the yard.

The last Monday in April seemed like the start of a normal work week as assignments were given out. The German crew was to continue work at the roundhouse as other crews worked in remote locations throughout the yard. But the actions of the German crew that day initiated a series of events that would later cause much excitement in the village and even in surrounding communities. A track laborer's wage was one dollar and ten cents for a ten hour day, roughly the equivalent of four dollars per hour today, so the wages being paid by the railroad were really terribly low. This was probably a subject discussed by the Germans after work on Saturday and as more beer was consumed, talk of a strike for higher wages probably took place. As they returned to work on Monday, the Germans demanded an increase of twenty-five cents more per day, threw down their shovels and quit working. Mr. Rouso refused to even talk about a raise and demanded the crew get to work or be discharged. They stood their ground and announced they were united in a strike against the railroad. Rouso's response was firm, announcing that they were all fired and instructing them to report to the paymaster for a final settlement. They thought he was bluffing and when the Germans showed up for work on Tuesday morning, they discovered that supervisor Rouso had a plan to complete the work required on the round house project without them. He had reassigned the Italian laborers to the project and they were in the process of laying track to the roundhouse. Throughout the morning, the Germans remained in the vicinity of the roundhouse and unsuccessfully attempted to convince the Italians to join them in a strike. The Germans thought their only chance of being rehired was a united work stoppage by all groups of laborers at Frankfort. There was a communication problem, but the response from the Italians was a unanimous agreement not to join the strike and to keep working.

At noon, the workers were entitled to a one-hour lunch break. Mr. Rouso allowed the Italians to use a track hand car to return to a shanty where they boarded, about a mile east of the railyard. The Germans, knowing the Italians would be gone for that much time, gathered up the pics, hammers and shovels being used to install rail and put them in one pile. When the Italians returned from lunch, they encountered the Germans preventing access to the tools and once again, demanding they join the strike. Again, the Italians refused to strike and moved toward the pile of tools. They gathered up ballast stones from the tracks and began hurling them at the Germans. They were encouraged by Mr. Rouso, who stood behind them, yelling in his deep, gruff voice "get your tools and get to work." Before long, both sides were throwing stones, bricks, and anything else available at each other.

The Germans were outnumbered and began to retreat.

The exception was Edward Heysner who drew a revolver and fired several shots over the heads of the Italians. Instead of quelling the fighting, the German's warning shots brought a volley of shots from the Italians who were also carrying concealed weapons. Mr. Rouso took refuge behind a railroad car and later recalled that about eight shots were fired during the melee. The gunfire was aimed wildly but one bullet did strike the German gunman Heysner, dropping him to the ground. The shot struck him in the head and would surely be fatal.

The Italians panicked upon seeing this, and threw off their coats and hats and removed the heavy work boots all were wearing as they scrambled to exit the yard, heading east, barefooted through the fields surrounding the shops. The yard was busy with other employees who either joined in the chase of the fleeing Italians or gave attention to the fallen German. Frankfort doctors Lehr and Richards were called and had the unconscious Heysner taken to his brother's house where he had been boarding. A bullet had entered the top of the victim's head and made a large hole his skull. The physicians removed fragments of his skull and did what they could, but the patient died at 6 p.m. that evening. When Coroner Warner was notified he immediately impaneled a jury and they viewed the remains before an inquest was to take place the following day.

The entire group of Italians fled and successfully evaded their pursuers. Police Justice H.H. Ingham contacted law enforcement in neighboring villages to have the fugitives intercepted. Five were captured quickly. One was running across the flats in Ilion, two were taken at Palmer's Grove and two were running along the south side of the Erie Canal at East Frankfort. At the time, it was believed the shooter was not one of them. The next day, three more of the workers that had fled were captured near Little Falls. By then it was believed that the lone fugitive captured in Ilion was probably the gunman. At the inquest trial he was identified by witnesses as the man who shot Edward Heysner.

Loftis Hall on Main Street was packed for the coroner's inquest. The shooting had caused much excitement in the village and residents were eager to hear testimony about the incident that resulted in the death of a man who had lived with his brother in the village for two years. District Attorney Steele conducted the interrogation of witnesses and Sheriff Brown was in charge of the Italians brought in from the Herkimer County Jail. As testimony got underway, witness accounts were consistent about events that occurred leading up to the shooting. All agreed that the Italians, being denied access to their work tools, started throwing objects at the Germans and Germans retaliated. But details about the actual shooting incident varied as to who initiated the gun battle, resulting in the death of Edward Heysner.

John Rouso, foreman of the yard, testified and gave details about the removal of the tools by the German crew, how the Germans guarded the pile of tools and how the Italians began the affray by throwing stones and other objects at the Germans. He identified the Italians by tag number but could not identify which crew member fired the deadly bullet. He claimed to have heard up to ten shots fired during the confrontation and said that when the group of Italians ran off to the east, he ran to Heysner and saw a revolver lying on the ground next to the wounded man. William Rekemeyer was closest to the victim at the time of the shooting and was confident that the Italian wearing tag number 5136 fired the fatal shot. Rouso identified the worker wearing 5136 as Alphonso Didano. When questioned about the confidence level of his testimony, Rekemeyer replied "I am positive it was him. I had seen 5136 at work many times. He is an uncouth looking, swarthy fellow with light hair and eyes, making his identification easy."

Tag number 5136, Alphonso Didano, took the stand and confirmed the testimony given, up to the stone throwing incident. He claimed the Germans started throwing stones first and said that the German, Heysner, pulled out a pistol and began firing. The five chamber revolver found near Heysner's unconscious body was displayed and Didano denied it was his.

Testimony was further complicated when eye witness Charles Wilson testified. He had been sitting in engine 37 and had a very good view of what occured. He claimed that another German, Albert Sommers, fired at the Italians and the Italians then shot at the Germans. Sommers was present and took the stand, claiming he did not have or fire a pistol. The conflicting stories presented on day one of the inquest cast doubt on the whole shooting matter. Some were unsure that Heysner had a pistol and thought Didono had thrown his weapon at Heysner after shooting him. Another likely reliable eyewitness, Frederick Desellas, worked for the yardmaster and saw the shooting incident unfold a short distance from where he was standing. He was certain of two things; he saw a German shoot a pistol in the direction of the Italians and

Alfonzo Didono was the shooter who fired at Edward Heysner. He described the fatal shooting in a manner that explained the angle the bullet took from the top of Heysner's head downward. He said that after Heysner shot his pistol at the Italians, he reached down to get something to hurl at the Italians and because of his bent-over position was hit in the head. The coroner agreed with that scenario.

By the time the coroner's inquest trial concluded on May 1, 1885, several witnesses had sworn that tag number 5136, Alphonso Didono, was the person who had inflicted the fatal wound upon Edward P. Heysner. The jury returned the following verdict:

> We find that Edward Heysner came to his death by concussion of the brain caused by a wound in the forehead caused by a bullet shot from a revolver in the hands of Alfonso Didono, No. 5136. We further say that in our estimation, Joseph N. Rouso deserves censure for not using proper efforts to prevent the affray which resulted in the shooting and death of Heysner.

Didono was returned to the Herkimer County Jail to await the determination of the grand jury. He joined twenty-five other prisoners that were being held for indictment including Francisa Mundone, (chapter 3) being held for the murder of John Wishart. The volume of arrests for serious crimes at the time filled the docket at the Herkimer County Courthouse and Didono sat in a jail cell nearly seven months before the grand jury heard his case. On November 18, 1885, the jury failed to indict him and he was released. He boarded a train for New York City and may have returned to Italy.

Before Didono was released, another incident occurred about one hundred yards east of the Frankfort passenger depot on Orchard Street, very close to where Edward Heysner was shot. On October 24, 1885, after a night of drinking, twenty-seven-year-old Harrison Winn and twenty-four-year-old Henry Hart returned to caboose 67 in the Frankfort railyard to get some sleep. Both Winn and Hart worked as brakemen on the West Shore Railroad and it was common for train personnel to use parked cabooses for overnight stays in the Frankfort repair shop yard. Several employees were staying in other cabooses that night. Winn lived in Oneonta and had a wife and infant child. Hart was unmarried and had a criminal record in his hometown of Schenectady.

Early Saturday morning, John Garvey, yardmaster at Frankfort, received word that there had been trouble during the night in one of the cabooses. He entered caboose 67 and found Harrison Winn lying in a pool of blood, unconscious. It was obvious from a trail of blood on the floor that he had moved about during the night and that his injuries had occurred several hours before being discovered. He had four deep gashes on the top of his head and in one spot a fracture of the skull could be seen. Dr. G.N. Lehr was called and the Frankfort physician held little hope that his patient would survive. Word spread throughout the community that a man had died, possibly murdered.

The weapon used was found on the floor of the caboose. An eighteen inch wooden club, made out of a pick handle, the type of handle used as a lever by train brakemen, was found covered with blood and hair. Dr. Lehr treated the fracture as best he could and hoped infection would not set in. During the morning Winn had bouts of consciousness and Justice H.H. Ingham was called to take an antemortem statement but the patient was again unconscious. Mr. Winn was moved to a nearby boarding house and his father was summoned from Oneonta to care for him.

Meanwhile, his bunk mate, Henry Hart was seen in downtown Frankfort. He went to the West Shore offices on East Main Street to see Mr. R.B. Williams, a trainmaster in charge of bookkeeping for the railroad. Hart wanted to know if he would be credited with a certain amount of time which he had lost previously while suffering from an injury. After discussing that matter for a short time, Mr. Williams asked: "Do you know that the man you hit in the head last night is dead?". Hart replied: "No; is he? Then I will go up street and give myself up to an officer." Mr. Williams told him that would be the best thing to do and asked how it happened. Hart replied: "I was lying on a couch in the caboose and Winn came in drunk and began picking a quarrel with me and threatened me with a club. We finally got into a wrestle and I threw him down. I then said I would quit if he would. He agreed and went to bed. Pretty soon Winn got up and commenced as before and flourished the club around my head. I grabbed the club and hit him twice with it over the head, and we both lay down again."

Mr. Williams felt the man was sincere and would deliver himself up to the Frankfort police but Hart disappeared and was nowhere to be found after talking to Williams. Hart had been in Frankfort about six months and when the Herkimer County Sheriff checked with the Schenectady Police

Department it was learned that they had issued a warrant for Mr. Hart earlier and that his brother was serving time in a Schenectady jail. The story Hart told Mr. Williams was all that authorities had until it was learned there was a witness to the crime. The witness was the person who informed Mr. Garvey (the man who discovered an unconscious Harrison Winn), that an incident had occurred during the night.

James Quinn was a young man barely out of his teens and had just started a career with the railroad. He was extremely frightened by what he'd seen and gave his account of the assault only when pressed by Sheriff Brown. Quinn was sleeping in a caboose adjacent to where Hart and Winn were staying and was awakened by noise around 2 a.m. A lantern was burning in the other caboose and Quinn could see and hear a man shouting: "I'll kill you, you son of a bitch." He saw the man raise a club above his shoulders with both hands and strike down upon another man he presumed to be on a couch. The man who assaulted the other got dressed and while doing so, walked back to the couch and looked at the victim, apparently to see what condition he was in. As the perpetrator turned down the lamp, Quinn was certain that the man had seen him watching from the other caboose. Quinn feared for his life, but the man left caboose 67 in another direction, only to return again after about twenty minutes had passed. A frightened Quinn waited until morning to notify Garvey of what he had witnessed.

Henry Hart evaded capture for three months, believing he had killed Harrison Winn. But Winn did not die from the attack. When later found in Troy, New York, Hart was arrested for first-degree assault and soon joined his brother in prison.

Chapter 5

A Bad Man from Frankfort 1900

Frankfort had a sizable group of citizens that were temperance minded and anti-saloon. They promoted and supported the prohibition of the sale of alcoholic beverages. The prominent Gates family, owners of Frankfort's largest industry prior to the West Shore Railroad shops coming to town, were very active in the temperance movement. William B. Gates, son of the match company's founder, was an annual delegate to the National Prohibition Convention. His brother, Frederick Gates, developed the idea to build a temperance city, Harriman, Tennessee, a city of over five thousand people. Before he left Frankfort, Fred was the Prohibition Party's candidate for New York State Secretary of State, held the state party's office of treasurer, and then president. The village's largest religious congregation during that time was the Methodist Episcopal group. They met in a large brick church on Main Street and strongly pushed temperance in the community. Beside religious guidance, perhaps the greatest motivator behind the movement was the actual cost to the community brought about by the abuse of alcohol. For two decades, beginning around the turn of the century in 1900, one family in Frankfort kept the legal system busy. The cause of each incident was related to the abuse of alcohol.

Henry Heath was born in Gouverneur, New York, but later brought to Frankfort during the area's boom days when the railroad shops were operating. For a man low in stature, he caused lawmen in Frankfort, Utica and Herkimer County an inordinately large amount of trouble. Described as being little, if any, over five feet in height but well-built at one hundred and thirty pounds, his small body probably contributed to his inability to handle liquor. Henry was described as handsome; light blue eyes, light hair and a sandy mustache. He attracted and married Sarah Leach, a Schuyler resident several years younger than he and before long they had five children.

Henry's problem with alcohol first surfaced in September 1900. School was starting and Henry set out to purchase schoolbooks for the children, taking the train to Utica. But the alcohol demon took over and instead of schoolbooks, Henry purchased whiskey and became extremely intoxicated to the point where he caused trouble on Utica's streets and was arrested for public intoxication. It was his first offense and a compassionate judge, listening to his story about his wife and five children at home, gave Henry a suspended sentence of sixty days. That brush with the legal system would be the first of many. Henry and Sarah became regulars in the saloons of Frankfort and the incidents that follow that lifestyle followed them. In September 1902, a skirmish resulted in Carlo DiPalmi (labeled as an "Italian from Utica") by newspapers of the day, being arrested for an assault on Sarah that was wisely interrupted by bystanders. She bore the marks of the injuries sustained and was completely prostrated when released from him. The attacker was captured by officers Getman and Seymour as he was leaving the village and placed in the lockup.

Sarah also began to be abused at home by Henry and eight months after being attacked by the Utican, Sarah felt the need to procure a peace warrant from the Frankfort police chief to protect her from Henry's wife-beating bouts. But she never appeared at a hearing and her failure to attend the hearing resulted in a dismissal of the warrant on Henry who was out on bond. Her desire to be protected from her husband went unfulfilled. One year later, in August 1904, a trip with their five children to attend a parade and circus in the city of Utica may have been Henry's meaculpa. Henry had accumulated extra money by working on the Percy Budlong farm in Schuyler. It was less than a year before that a tragic shooting death had occurred on the farm. Herbert Moon, a twelve year old from Utica had been in trouble at an industrial school so his father brought him to the farm to work during summer vacation. But trouble followed him to the farm where he began a daily conflict with twenty-year-old Lucien Drew, a simple-minded fellow originally from Michigan. Young Moon carried a rifle and had been warned by several adults to be careful with it after he had shown to be reckless, often shooting at trees or items around the farm. On September 3, 1903 another argument occurred between the two young farmhands and Moon chased Drew with the gun, firing wildly into the air. Tragically, one bullet struck Drew in the head, killing him. The lad, not yet a teenager, was deeply remorseful but the youngster was carted off to the Herkimer County Jail. After the incident Mr. Budlong needed help to maintain the dairy and Henry Heath was hired.

The Heath family boarded a trolley car to the city that warm August Friday morning and had plenty of time to spare before the circus parade would take place on Genesee Street. There was also enough time to depart at Stop 3 near the West Frankfort area known as Harbor; probably a planned stop to have a drink with the regulars at John Halwick's Hotel bar. But they did leave in time to catch the parade and a performance of the circus, leaving a baby carriage at the hotel, which of course would provide a reason to stop at the hotel on the return trip. Other watering holes in the city were visited and by the time the family was ready to return home, Henry was very intoxicated. They departed the trolley car at Stop 3 and returned to the bar at Halwick's late in the day. Sarah tended the children and Henry continued his day-long drinking bout.

Darkness came and Henry took the baby carriage from the hotel and headed toward the roadway. His family waited some time for his return until Sarah decided to continue home, thinking she must have lost her husband in the darkness. She walked to the area of the Mohawk River dyke, her children following closely by. As the group was passing by the dyke, Sarah saw Henry lying near the road, sound asleep. She called for him to wake up and take the children home with her and that was the point where Henry's day-long over-consumption of alcoholic beverages would result in life changing consequences that would affect the lives of he and his family.

He awakened as if possessed by demons, grabbed Sarah, threw her to the ground, kicked at her head, punched at her face and with their small children as witnesses, generally pounded his wife into insensibility. As the children fled he dragged his wife's bleeding body to the roadside. One of the children, Flora, only five years old, made her way back to the hotel and told her terrible story to several men in the barroom. They immediately rushed to the dyke area and located Sarah lying on the ground and bleeding. George Thomas, a large young man from Utica carried Sarah's lifeless body back to the hotel. Dr. Hayes of Frankfort was summoned and meanwhile, Henry was nowhere to be found.

Upon his arrival, Dr. Hayes found his patient in convulsions and with a cut in her lip extending from one nostril to her mouth, a badly bruised left temple, bruised right arm and head and body marks from blows or kicks. Frankfort Chief of Police Getman was notified and at that point, the outlook for her survival was poor. Sarah was brought to Faxton Hospital in Utica and Dr. Hayes continued attending to her there, along with Dr. Douglas of Utica. Dr. Hayes was coroner at the time and took an antemortem statement from his patient, verifying that her husband was the perpetrator. The logical opinion at that time was that she would probably die and the case would turn into one of manslaughter. But Sarah started to recover and by Tuesday doctors told the press there was a possibility she would survive.

The children were cared for by friends and relatives. The two older boys went with their grandfather, Noah Leach, in Schuyler and the youngest, a boy and two girls were taken to the Village of Frankfort to be cared for by Mrs. Susan Graves.

Chief Getman and Officer Storms found Henry at home the next morning and placed him under arrest. He had sobered up, but amazingly, seemed unsympathetic to his wife's condition. District Attorney Ward of Herkimer arrived and issued a warrant for assault in the first degree. Justice Piper of Frankfort committed Henry to the Herkimer County Jail to await the action of a grand jury. Henry pled not guilty. The feeling against Henry in Herkimer County at this point was very high. His previous assaults on Sarah while under the influence of alcohol had been reported in the local papers. An examination of the Heath home revealed a condition of filth and poverty hardly to be imagined. A few dishes, two hard chairs, two cots with straw bedding, and a wooden bench were the only furnishings. One fairly good stove was in use, but no food was found in the home.

One could guess that this story might be over. Henry goes to prison, reforms and comes home to be a sober and good father and husband. Not Henry Heath. The chapter title is taken from the headline printed in the *Utica Daily Press* on July 25, 1906, almost two years after the beating took place:

A BAD MAN FROM FRANKFORT

Just what caused such a determination? Henry sat in a jail cell from the day he was arrested in August 1904 until October 1st. A grand jury wasn't scheduled to meet until December to hear his case but Henry had his own plan to return to society. Sometime between Friday morning and Saturday afternoon, Henry sawed his way out of the Herkimer County Jail. Being a little guy helps in these matters and by cutting only one iron cross-bar over a window, making a foot square opening, he was able to escape.

Henry's disappearance from the jail was noticed when another prisoner about to be released from custody told the jailer that he had heard someone sawing the day before. An investigation found the sawed bar lying on the ground under the second story window. The jailer notified the Sheriff and the two made an inspection of the entire building. In Henry's cell, a man was lying on a cot and the two moved on to inspect other cells. Later, Henry's cell was examined again and it was empty. No one seemed to know exactly when the prisoner escaped or why he was observed in his cell earlier that day. Officials in Utica and the valley communities were notified to be on the lookout for the escaped man. The sheriff and another officer went to Utica on a search mission, knowing Henry had a friend there who had earlier posted bond for him. Also, a letter written to his wife by Henry, had been sent to a Utica address. During the search, Henry's mother was observed drunk on Whitesboro Street in the city and some believed that Henry had visited her and gave her whiskey. She denied she had seen him. Meanwhile, Frankfort police kept a close watch on the house where Sarah was living.

Speculation began on how Henry had obtained a hacksaw blade while in jail and information provided by the jailer proved truly amazing. He said that after recovering from the beating, Sarah was reconciling with her husband and had visited him at the jail twice. Many people concluded that she brought him a saw blade but others surmised he may have taken one from a contractor that was working on the building during the time of Henry's incarceration. Sheriff Austin Klock was disturbed that the escape happened under his watch and vowed to personally apprehend his nemesis,

Henry Heath. As fall ended in 1904 it seemed liked Klock's retribution would not come to fruition and when winter was almost done in 1905, no sign of Henry was found. But then on March 4th, Police Chief Austin Wilcox of the City of Oneida, New York, contacted Sheriff Klock and requested the sheriff get on the next train to Oneida where he could identify a man held in custody and believed to be Henry Heath.

The man being held by Oneida police said his name was Henry Clifford Hines and claimed that he had never been in Herkimer, New York. He protested his being detained and demanded that he be released. The man was aboard a New York Central train and had been tabbed as the escapee by railroad detective James Landers. The detective said he had met Henry Heath four years ago and was positive Mr. Hines was actually Heath. Mr. Hines was about five-foot-tall and his appearance matched a wanted poster, but even after Chief Wilcox held the man, his identity was in doubt and he urged Sheriff Klock to get to Oneida as soon as possible. Anxious to finally nab the man that embarrassed him and his jail staff, the sheriff arrived on the 2 p.m. train and was taken to the cell holding Mr. Hines. Seeing the Herkimer County Sherrif, Mr. Hines said "Hello, sheriff." "Hello, Henry Heath," replied Klock as he took his man into custody, assuring Chief Wilcox that Henry Heath would never escape his jail again.

Once his identity was established, Henry thought of himself as a folk hero as he was surrounded by reporters from big city newspapers, grilling him about how he had remained in the area and avoided being recognized. Little five-foot-tall Henry became quite boisterous about telling his story, giving out details of his escape freely. He claimed the saw blades used to cut the window bar had actually been smuggled into the jail by another inmate who then got "cold feet" about sawing his way out. He said he probably wouldn't have attempted an escape if only Sarah had come to visit him. If true, that made the jailer's story that Sarah had visited Henry and probably brought the saw blades to him, false.

Henry was again interviewed by reporters after the positive identification and disseminated every detail of his activities during the months when he was "on the lam." He even claimed that he "could have gotten away" in Oneida but chose not to. He had been all over the state, hopping on trains and traveling by rail by, "riding between the tender and front car." He worked in Syracuse, Fulton and Buffalo, "riding the canal and had a great time." He said he was drunk only twice and was taken before Judge Wilson in Fulton who let him go, telling him not to get drunk again and he claimed he didn't. In Syracuse he was questioned by several policemen and gave a false identity. Before he was caught in Oneida he had been in Little Falls and bought shoes there; at Herkimer, he walked over the West Canada Creek Bridge, and then visited Whitesboro and Oriskany. He claimed he spoke to a constable from Marcy who knew who he was. His last statement summed up his view of the escape: "I never did anything without knowing what I was doing. I was feeling pretty good, I tell you, but for Sheriff Klock I would have got away. Well here I am Sheriff, take me away, I'm ready to take what is coming to me." Back in the Herkimer County Jail, Henry gave the details of his escape to Sheriff Klock and showed him two other ways that he could have escaped if he was unable to saw through the steel window bar.

Within two weeks, Henry Heath, alias Henry Hines was sent to Auburn State Prison to serve a year and a half at hard labor. At Auburn, he was said to be a model prisoner and the parole board released him in July 1906, two months before his term would expire in September. Henry returned to Frankfort and his old habits. During a drinking episode at Bargy's Bar he proclaimed that he had returned to Frankfort for one reason; to kill both Chief of Police Getman and Coroner Dr. Hayes, the two men involved in the arrest that led to his imprisonment. Doctor Hayes did not take the threat as being innocuous. He considered Henry Heath capable of such a deed and immediately went before Justice Ingham and swore out a warrant for Henry's arrest. Sheriff Klock willingly notified Auburn Prison authorities of the parole violation. Henry sat in the county jail until a hearing was held and this time he voluntarily pled guilty and was sent back to prison for one year. Herkimer County took charge of his children.

Henry rejoined his wife Sarah after again being released early from Auburn and this time he made no further threats to people involved in previous episodes of his activities. But he returned to drinking and was still unable to "handle his booze." Within three years of his release he made another attack on Sarah. On August 23, 1909, in a drunken rage, he hit her in the face with a flatiron, breaking her nose and kicking her while she lay bleeding and unconscious on the floor, breaking her ribs. Frankfort Chief of Police Johnson was summoned and upon his arrival witnessed Henry still kicking Sarah. In trying to subdue the senseless attacker, the chief threw a blow at Henry with his fist, breaking two bones in his hand in doing so.

Sarah was beaten as badly as in the attack five years earlier and again it was possible she would not survive. But as the days went by, Dr. Albones thought she would recover while under his treatment. Once again, Henry was arrested for first degree assault and committed to the Herkimer County Jail to wait the action of the next grand jury. Henry was indicted for second degree assault and in January 1910 a trial was held.

The outcome of the assault trial was to be expected. Henry the wife-beater was again sentenced to hard labor at Auburn Prison for a term of one year. But the seemingly short sentence in view of his criminal record came about because of Sarah. District Attorney Schmidt called Sarah as a witness against her husband and people in the courtroom could not believe what was happening. She was very unwilling to give any testimony against her husband. She had to be cautioned several times by the court to answer the district attorney's questions or be held in contempt. She finally stated that her injuries that day were caused by her falling on the front steps of the Heath's home. Henry's verdict was determined and Sarah was charged with perjury and jailed. Three of the Heath children were placed in institutions in Syracuse and the remaining two were placed in the care of Miss Brownell of the State Charities Aid Association. Sarah remained in jail for over a month until bail was posted on a bond signed by H.H. Ingham and William Wayne of Frankfort.

After his release from prison again, Henry and Sarah still made the newspapers now and then. In September of 1912 Henry and another man, Edward Quale, went to a doctor's office to be treated for some slight knife wounds. Police investigated and the two claimed to be the victims of highway robbers who stopped them and put revolvers to their heads before Henry and his companion fought them off, sustaining the cuts.

Frankfort and Herkimer County had the good fortune of the Heath clan moving to the City of Utica around 1913 but could still keep up with their accomplishments by reading the Utica papers:

In July 1919 Henry and Sarah were arrested for keeping a disorderly house on Blandina Street. $10 or 10 days in jail. In the prohibition years that followed, the lack of legal alcohol made no changes to their lifestyle.

In May 1923 Sarah was struck in the forehead and cut by a plate that somehow had slipped out of Henry's hand. She required hospital attention. The judge, blaming both, sentenced her to thirty days and him to sixty days. Sarah's plea "Let me go home and I'll vote for you judge" was ignored.

In 1924 both were sentenced to the Oneida County Jail for five days for public intoxication.

In July 1925 Sarah was able to sway a judge in City Court. After Judge Buckley said he might sentence her to a stay in a Troy, New York jail, Sarah said to the very well acquainted justice, "Oh, judge, have a heart, I wouldn't do that to you." Her probation officer then told the judge that he needed pea pickers in his program at a local farm. Without hesitation, Sarah shouted out, "I'm a pea picker, judge, I just came back from a farm where Henry and I were picking peas." Judge

Buckley laughed, but sentenced Sarah to spend fifteen days in a local jail.

In 1929, during the Christmas holidays, and before prohibition was repealed, Henry Heath died of a heart attack in the home of his son Floyd on Oriskany Street West in Utica.

Chapter 6

The Black Hand Societies 1905

A reign of terror existed in the Village of Frankfort from about 1905 until the early 1920s. A migration from Calabria, Italy and Sicily brought with it a small group of men belonging to Black Hand Societies that were prevalent in the old world. My book, Stories Forgotten Frankfort, N.Y., included several examples of how the societies extorted money from Italian and Sicilian immigrants who had come to the village or the surrounding area earlier, obtaining decent jobs or purchasing farms. They found a more rewarding lifestyle in their new country but became targets of the Black Handers simply because they were successful. As explained in my previous book, these desperadoes threatened Italian-speaking immigrants and not the majority of "American" residents. The same plan was being carried out throughout the country. The extortion plot that demanded James DeLuke place one thousand dollars in a barrel in Frankfort, followed exactly the instructions given to a wealthy Italian liquor dealer in Buffalo, New York whose life was threatened unless he left one thousand dollars in a barrel on the canal towpath in Buffalo.

The Black Handers were young men in their twenties and some of them were treacherous. The oath administered to new members of the Black Hand Society is in itself an example of why the decent immigrant was intimidated:

The candidate draws blood from his own body and smears that blood on the image of his favorite saint. The bloody image is then burned and as it burns he takes the following oath:

"I swear on my honor to be faithful to the brotherhood. As this saint and the drops of my blood are destroyed, so will I shed all my blood for the fraternity; and as these ashes and this blood can never be restored, so can I never become free from the brotherhood."

He then shoots at a crucifix to signify his readiness to kill even his nearest relative if bidden by the society.

The impact of receiving a letter of extortion, and the retribution that would follow if the victim went to authorities, was life changing. After Frank John, a highly respected Italian farmer residing in the reservation, took a note that demanded one thousand dollars of him to the Herkimer County Sheriff, three men were arrested and sent to prison. Following their trial, Mr. John's three horses were killed in a fire that burned his barns to the ground; a fire that was set in the middle of the night. And after the retaliation upon Mr. John, things only got worse in the village.

Around midnight On October 4, 1907, Joseph Dinardo a man who had only been in Frankfort for nine months and was working as a painter, but was known to be a member of one of the Black Hand societies, was murdered on the front stoop of a house on Sheldon Avenue where he rented a room. The owner of the boarding house was a brother of Tony Guiliano, who was serving six years at hard labor in Auburn prison after being found guilty along with John DeCaro in the Frank John extortion attempt.

The murder was not reported until six a.m. Two men living in the house had left to go to work at the Ilion typewriter factory before that time, yet when questioned said they knew nothing and had heard no shots during the night. In fact, a total of eight men lived in the house and when all were arrested on suspicion, every man claimed not to have seen or heard anything. Police had been called to the scene by the owner of the building. He had placed an old overcoat over the body. The murdered man was last seen at Lombardo's Saloon on Orchard Street around 10:30 p.m. The murder weapon was determined to be a shotgun when it was discovered that four heavy pieces of lead had entered DiNardo's back and had come out through his chest along with other pellets that had entered his arms. The location of the shooter was presumed to be in a cornfield directly across the street and only fifty feet from the front stoop where the body was found. It was speculated that someone called to DiNardo in the rain that night, and upon seeing no one, he was re-entering the house when he was shot in the back. He had no shoes on. Pieces of lead were found in the door and the door casing so it was very easy for Coroner Hayes to determine that the deadly weapon was a shotgun and any of the shots that entered the body could have caused the victim's death. One had passed through the heart and others had perforated the liver and lungs. At the inquest it was speculated that the shot could have been intended for another resident of the house, but that was never determined and the murderer was never caught.

There was a consensus in the Italian community that the murder was a vendetta by friends of Frank John and others who had received extortion letters. It was thought that an Italian who was not a member of the Black Hand, or who was at least a sympathizer with those that had been victims of the societies, waited his chances and during a heavy rain that night, filled DiNardo full of lead. Sheriff Klock of Herkimer, along with Frankfort Chief of Police Getman and Under Sheriff Firth began a futile investigation; nobody in the Italian section knew anything about the murder. When the Herkimer County Board of Supervisors offered a five hundred dollar reward for information leading to the capture of the criminals involved in the Frankfort cases, a Little Falls Times editorial sharply criticized the resolution, saying Frankfort alone should take on the elimination of the Black Hand just as Little Falls and Herkimer had done.

Only two months had passed after the DiNardo murder when Joseph Dove gunned down Giuseppe Skran on Frankfort's Main Street. The details of the shooting were fully covered in the Stories Forgotten book. Here's a quick recap: The Dove family had been victimized by a group of Black Handers. As usual, the game was extortion. They demanded a payment of three hundred dollars within three days. The amount was dropped to two hundred dollars when Dove said he didn't have and couldn't raise that kind of money. Two hundred dollars back then was equal to five thousand dollars today. With the threat of a large knife, Mr. and Mrs. Dove were told that each would be beheaded and their house blown up if they didn't turn over the money on time. Dove went to Chief of Police Getman with his story and was given the chief's permission to arm himself and protect his family until the extortionists were dealt with by the authorities. The three day time period arrived and Dove was followed to Main Street by Giuseppe Skran who demanded the payment. Dove's payment consisted of three bullets fired into Skran's chest. Skran ran to Lombardo's Saloon on Orchard Street where he died.

Dove was arrested and went to trial. The Herkimer County Grand Jury listened to Dove's story and acquitted him on all charges. An incident that undoubtedly helped Dove was a robbery committed by Skran on Railroad Street. After Skran was killed, an Italian who had come to Frankfort from Schenectady only ten days before the shooting contacted the Frankfort police and said Skran led five other men that had robbed him at gunpoint near the railroad crossing. When he refused to give them money he was assaulted and the thirty dollars he carried taken from him. Now that Skran was dead, the victim was emboldened to come forward because he saw Skran as the leader of the group. The jury's failure to indict Dove came under sharp criticism from Judge Ward, who said there was no justification for a jury's failure to indict a man who had shot down another. A newspaper headline proclaimed "It's not a crime to kill a Black Hand agent in Frankfort." Prosecutors attempted to bring others involved in the extortion attempt to justice, but had little success. One man who was at Dove's house when the extortion threat was made was brought before the jury. Carmello Carnigliaro was charged with first-degree attempted robbery but his testimony and lack of any reliable witnesses led to all charges being dropped. He testified that he was not present when the demand for money was made and was at Dove's house by invitation of Dove's brother-in-law. He had just come to Frankfort in July after serving in the Italian Army.

But just as Frank John had lost his horses and barns to the Black Hand extortionists, the Dove family suffered a fate far worse than losing material possessions. The family had been in this country only three years before Dove felt the necessity to shoot the extortionist Skran and after he killed the Black Hand member, life in America proved anything but rewarding. The society felt Joseph Dove had betrayed them in three ways. He had killed their fraternity brother Giuseppe Scran, he had given the authorities information on members of the fraternity, leading to the arrest of some of them, and of course, he had refused their demand for money. The family of eight feared for their lives daily. Good friends were said to look out for and even act as bodyguards for Joseph Dove as he left the house daily to work at his job in Ilion at Remington Arms. Many noticed that one of his sons walked several feet behind him when Dove had someplace to go. He had armed the older boys with revolvers. When one of the sons was arrested in Utica for carrying both a gun and a knife he was released without charges after telling the judge his story.

Shades were always drawn in the Dove home and it was noticeable that the home was barricaded every night in fear of a Black Hand threat. Within a few months of Dove's acquittal for the Skran shooting, threatening letters with the infamous black hand marking were placed near the front steps of the Dove home. They were blood money letters demanding payments that could be made in installments and would afford the family protection from retribution. When Dove again chose to ignore the threats by not placing money as instructed, a series of incidents began to occur in July 1908.

One night, as darkness approached, Joseph Dove heard a noise and upon investigating found a pile of wood shavings and a pail of kerosene in the front hallway leading into the house. The intruders fled and Dove reported to the police that someone had attempted an arson that could have killed his entire family. It was only a week after that incident that Dove's son, Carl went to the front door after hearing noises and was confronted by a group that he knew to be Black Hand members. One of the group slashed at the teenager and inflicted a knife wound to the boy's shoulder. Officers Farley and Williams took a statement from Carl that included the names of all five visitors.

The officers were quick to arrest Tony Martino and Steve Mangora, but not easily. The two pretended to be asleep in beds at their boarding house. When a flashlight was turned on Martino he reached for his revolver, but was taken without incident as the two officers pointed their guns at him. The police then rounded up the remaining three hoodlums. After a grand jury session, all but Mangora were released. He was tried for assault. This group had also been active in other extortion attempts that included one where protection money was paid to them by the Minosh family.

The constant fear of retribution by members of the Black Hand societies took a huge toll on the Dove family. Mrs.

Dove's health was affected by a nervous condition that made her fear any stranger. Reporters attempted to interview her without success. She was admitted to a hospital in Utica and eventually died two years after her son Carl was stabbed. She was only forty-two years old. The father, Joseph Dove died in 1920 at the age of fifty-four. His son, Joseph, died three years later. He was only twenty years old. A daughter, Rose, who raised her brothers after Mrs. Dove passed, died in 1927 at the age of twenty-six. Carl had several brushes with the legal system and spent six months in the Onondaga County Penitentiary in 1931. He died six years later at the age of forty-five.

In the same time period when Joseph Dove killed Giuseppe Skran, other families in the area of Sheldon Avenue were being terrorized by young men who had joined one of the Black Hand societies. One extortion plot ended in another shooting of a Black Hand leader. In October 1907, two months before the Skran shooting, Monano Romano began threatening the family of Dominick Minosh. Two hundred and fifty dollars was demanded and that amount was paid by Mr. Minosh's wife, Rose.

Emboldened by the ease at which money was obtained, Romano, who had also been involved in terrorizing the Dove's, made demands to Minosh but was told there was no more money for him. He came to the Minosh home in March 1908, with four others and demanded fifty dollars, or Mr. Minosh's eyes "would be put out if the money was not forthcoming." But after he made the October payment, Dominick Minosh armed himself to protect his family. He was permitted to carry a gun by the Frankfort police.

When Romano completed his demand for immediate payment, Minosh wasted no time in pulling out his revolver and shooting three bullets into Romano. Luckily (for Romano) one of his accomplices reached out and deflected Minosh's aim, preventing shots to the body that would have proven fatal. Two bullets entered an ankle and one grazed a cheek. Romano was not severely injured, and ran from the scene toward the West Shore Railroad offices. Frank Seamans, an employee of the railroad, heard the shots and saw the man running. He immediately gave chase, overtook and captured the wounded man. Chief Getman and Officer Clarke took Romano into custody and later found and arrested Romano's four accomplices. One of the four, Joseph Simonette, was said to be close to Romano in the hierarchy of the Black Hand.

Before the Minosh affray and after Dove shot Skran, Romano had been evading authorities by staying with a brother in Rome, N.Y., only returning to Frankfort to extort Minosh. The immigrant colony in was relieved when Herkimer County Court Judge Ward sent Romano to Auburn State Prison in May 1908 for a term not less than two or for more than six years. Joseph Simonette claimed he acted as an accomplice to Romano only out of fear for his own life if he did not follow orders. D.A. Lewis made a positive statement regarding the defendant, saying Simonette had been open and frank in his confession to him and said he did not believe the man was a criminal at heart. But Judge Ward imposed a sentence of at least one year in Auburn State Prison, lecturing the defendant about being more careful as to who he associated with. Simonette wept, saying he would help catch the Black Hand. His wife and four children looked on.

Sending black hand participants to prison slowed extortion activity in Frankfort and encouraged immigrant groups to assimilate and be more forthcoming with the community. In the second decade of the 1900s crimes similar to those reported in the five-year period following 1905 decreased but authorities knew threats were still occurring. On Friday, June 27, 1913 a reminder would come that a few bad apples still roamed Frankfort streets.

Salvatore Versaro came from Sicily as a teenager and lived with adopted parents on Third Avenue. He was an intelligent, good-looking young man who was quickly learning to speak the English language. He started working for a company that was a contractor for the Utica and Mohawk Valley Railroad Company, the company running trolley lines throughout the valley. Versaro's talents were recognized by the contractor and soon he was put in charge of a group of Italian laborers who were paving areas between and alongside the rails. As a twenty-two-year-old foreman he now had a position that paid him a considerably higher wage than the fellow countrymen working under him were earning. With that fact came jealousy, leading to attempted extortion by those following the mindset of the criminal element.

Sam Versaro (as he was now called) was making plans for his future with money he had been saving. He had sent money to a woman in the old country who was to be his bride. She was on her way to Frankfort on a steamer when Sam went to Chief of Police Keller and reported that he was receiving threats written in Italian demanding a share of his savings. But when asked to supply the names of those threatening him, he said he couldn't do that out of fear that he would be killed. Chief Keller advised him to defend himself, the same recommendation, given years earlier to Joseph Dove before he killed Black Hand member Giuseppe Skran.

Around 8 p.m. on Friday, June 27, 1913, a group of men met Sam at Third Avenue and the group, including Sam, went to the woods on the reservation side of Reese Road. They were observed by several residents. Nobody saw the group return to the village. Sam's foster parents were excited that he had not come home Friday night. As a search was being organized, a group of Italian children from the reservation area discovered the body of a man in the Reese Road woods. The terrified children returned to their parents and reported what they had found. Chief Keller was notified and reported to the scene as did coroner Getman and Herkimer County Sheriff Stitt. The location of the body was outside the village limits and came under jurisdiction of the county. Nothing considered evidence was found in the vicinity of the body but Chief Getman had something in his possession to track the assailant or assailants. Getman and Charles Brickwood, Frankfort Village Electrician, were the owners of bloodhounds. They had been used in a large area around Frankfort and had been successful in tracking all types of criminals, even chicken thieves.

The dogs were taken to the crime scene and quickly headed east, hot on a trail they had picked up. They were let run and even Chief Keller had doubts about the trail after following the dogs over two miles. But the dogs led the chief to a small building at the Doty berry patch at Barringer Road in Ilion. In that building were four young Italian men. Salvatore Gillio, Francisco Macrio, Tony Russo and Carmelo Conzellis were taken into custody at gunpoint, arrested and taken to the Frankfort lockup located in the rear of the fire station. When questioned, a unanimous consensus emerged. Every man said that a fifth man, Charles Macrio plotted to rob Sam, robbed him at gunpoint of one hundred and fifty dollars and a gold watch, and then fired a bullet at point blank range into the man's chest. They had forced Sam to walk to the woods where the crime was committed by Macrio, who, upon seeing that he had killed a man, fled. The four remaining at the scene panicked and ran towards Ilion without a plan of what they were going to do. The autopsy revealed that a bullet had struck Sam's heart.

The four prisoners were transferred to the Herkimer County Jail where they were again questioned, and once again, all four told the same story. They were released and told they would have to testify at a grand jury hearing. But no indictment was ever brought against the shooter, Charles Macrio. He was never apprehended and probably returned to Italy or Sicily. Chief Keller, however, was moved by the fact that a good young Sicilian immigrant, about to be married, had come to him for help but lost his life because of greed and jealousy. Keller began a proactive approach right after the murder to rid the young immigrant community of weapons. The following appeared in the local newspaper a few months after the murder:

> *Chief Keller and his force are keeping a close watch over pool rooms and saloons in Frankfort. A thorough search was made Saturday for any foreigners carrying concealed weapons, examining a hundred persons.*

Chapter 7

Two Gun Sam 1910 – 1940

The generation growing up in Frankfort at the beginning of the twentieth century witnessed the exploits of Salvatore Polizzi, a man born in St. Joseph, Sicily in 1881. He came to America in 1906, settling in Brooklyn, New York, but was there for only six weeks before moving to Frankfort. The twenty-four-year-old young immigrant was joined by his wife Rosa and their young son, fourteen months later. They lived where a majority of immigrants had settled, the area north of Main Street encompassed by Sheldon Avenue, Railroad Street and Orchard Street, all just a short walk from the village's train depot where they had arrived from New York City. Sam, as he would be called in this country, proved to be a hard worker and provided for his family well. But Sam's life in his new country would be anything but stable. The family was joined by Rosa's brother, Pavalo Palermo, who moved in with the Polizzi's upon his arrival in Frankfort and was obligated to pay board for his living quarters. In October 1910 the issue of Pavalo "being behind in his rent" surfaced.

The rent issue escalated between Sam and his brother-in-law to a point where neighbors on Sheldon Avenue heard a threatening verbal exchange in Italian taking place between the two that might have led to an altercation or more. As it turned out, it was more than just a fist fight. Nineteen-year-old Pavalo pulled a pistol out of his pocket and fired once at Sam. He was apparently inexperienced in using a gun and his aim was terrible, missing Sam entirely, but hitting his sister who was standing by her husband. The bullet entered her breast and the bloody wound appeared very serious. Panic overcame the threesome and the immediate issue was to get medical attention for the bleeding sister and wife.

Police were summoned and Doctor Albones rushed to provide aid. He dressed the wound and discovered that the bullet had not penetrated further than the breast. Bleeding was stopped and everyone was elated that Rosa's survival seemed probable. That was good news, but Pavalo's actions brought him a spot in the Frankfort lockup, a hearing before Justice of the Peace George W. Jones, a transfer to the Herkimer County Jail and finally an indictment by the Herkimer County Grand Jury. This would be the first incident in Sam Polizzi's life involving a gun, but certainly would not be the last.

Twenty-one months after Sam was spared the bullet of his wife's brother, he attended a party in honor of a woman who was engaged to be married. The party included musician friends and was held at Ludovico Smizzi's house on Orchard Street, down the street from the Polizzi residence. One of the musicians was Joseph Agietto, who had been involved in an altercation with Sam Polizzi six months earlier. His brother, John

Agietto had also been involved in an intense argument with Polizzi just a day before at Jim DeLuke's Saloon on Litchfield Street. In that affray, Chief of Police John Johnson was summoned, but upon his arrival, both parties had fled the scene. At the party, Sam Polizzi noticed that Joe Agietto was playing a guitar and asked Mr. Smizzi, the host, if Joe was an invited guest. The reply was to the effect that the man playing the guitar was not an invited guest. Joe Agietto took exception to the answer and struck Sam Polizzi in the face. In an instant, an altercation began, just as had occurred six months previous, but several people in the room broke up the fight before it escalated. Joe Agietto left through the front door and Polizzi went outside, using the back door.

The party broke up and Polizzi went around to the front of the house to escort his wife home. Joe was gone down the street and it appeared that any further trouble between the two angry men was avoided. But that would not be the case. Joe Agietto's brother, John, fresh from the fight with Sam the night before, heard about the trouble at the party and showed up on the street just as Sam and his wife were departing. He confronted Sam about the trouble with his brother and Sam said to forget it, he'd had a few drinks. But John grabbed Sam by the shoulders to once again begin an altercation and again, the pair was separated by bystanders.

Polizzi and his wife started down Sheldon Avenue toward home. The following story is told in the words of Sam Polizzi himself, years later. Other witnesses were his wife and his sister Mary Piazza. John Agietto sprung from behind a tree with a stiletto in his hand and lunged at Sam, striking him in his left arm. Sam cried out "John, stop, stop." But he did not stop, lunging at Sam again as he yelled "no, you no good son of a bitch, I'll kill you!" Sam turned and ran a few yards with John in pursuit. It was then that Sam pulled a revolver from his pocket and fired two shots at John that stopped the knife-wielding aggressor and allowed Sam to run home. Agietto ran down Sheldon Avenue in the opposite direction, reaching the corner at Frankfort Street. Polizzi would later claim that he never saw John fall as he reached the corner.

Neighbors left their houses to help the fallen man and Doctors Richards and Hayes were summoned. Rev. Joseph Granna, pastor of the Italian Methodist Mission took Agietto to the new Ilion Hospital. At the hospital, both doctors agreed there was little chance for survival as each of the two bullets were lodged deep in different lungs. No attempt could be made to probe for the bullets due to the damage inflicted. They summoned Coroner Getman and District Attorney Schmidt, who took an antemortem statement from the victim with the aid of an interpreter, taking a statement naming Polizzi as the shooter but little else. Agietto did say that he was standing on the street near Polizzi's home, talking to a man named Caruso, when Salvatore Polizzi came along and without warning opened fire on him. Agieto lived two blocks from where the shooting occurred.

Chief John Johnson went to Polizzi's home after Agietto was taken to the hospital and found only the shooter's wife and child. Polizzi had gone to a neighbor's house to have his arm bandaged. Johnson knew Sam was in hiding and immediately put out full-description bulletins to surrounding communities; Salvatore Polizzi, Italian, about five feet, nine inches tall, weight about one hundred and sixty pounds, about thirty-five years old (he was thirty), black mustache, dark eyes and hair. Three days went by without a sighting when John Agietto died in the hospital and was later buried in Potter's Field in the Oak View Cemetery. Salvatore Polizzi was now a fugitive, wanted for first degree murder. The initial bit of information on Polizzi's escape had him taking the trolley to Utica. After that came little information on his whereabouts and after several years the case was almost forgotten. Frankfort already had two cases where a murderer was never apprehended and it began to look like this one would be added to that list.

Five months after John Agietto died, the Herkimer County Grand Jury heard the evidence and on December 12, 1912, indicted the missing man for first degree murder. But it was over nine years before Salvatore Polizzi would be captured and have to answer that charge. It was probably the fact that Herkimer County had several cases to be solved during the same time period that would lead to Sam's arrest. The county engaged Detective Michael Bernabic of New York City to chase down Polizzi and others. The big city detective was on the Frankfort fugitive's trail for many months and the following information was provided to the court by him.

Polizzi did take the trolley heading to Utica but departed west of the village and stayed at a friend's farmhouse for two days. He then went to the home of an uncle, John Lucci, at 152 Lock Street in Rome, New York. Again, he only stayed with his uncle two days before taking the train to Windsor, Wisconsin, outside of Madison. There was a small Italian colony there and he hid amongst them for two and a half years. He left because Joseph Agietto, the brother of the man Sam shot, showed up in Wisconsin. Sam was sure he was there to revenge his brother's murder. He took the train to Los Angeles, California and was there for two years. A rumor (never proven) circulated that while in California, Polizzi killed a man from New Haven, Connecticut who had fled to California after killing a man back in New Haven. Sam returned to Rome and was hired by the Rome Brass and Copper Company. It was easy to blend in with the many Italian-born workers there. At the time, over two hundred and fifty immigrants worked in the mill.

Sam's stay in Rome was shortened by rumors that the authorities were after him. He was sure that Detective Bernabic was in the city and, after his eventual capture, said he had spotted the detective more than once. He fled Rome quickly and left the job at the copper mill without drawing his pay, which, in those days was paid in cash. He then joined associates that were in the bootlegging business in New Haven, Connecticut and while he was there, a murder was committed. This was one more murder close to Polizzi and the coroner demanded that New Haven authorities hold him as a material witness. But Sam escaped the law again and joined a friend in Brooklyn, New York. It was now almost nine years after the Frankfort shooting and Sam boldly returned to Frankfort where he had four sisters and a brother. He was now using the names Leonardo D'Martini or D'Piazzi.

Polizzi knew Detective Bernabic was in Herkimer at different times so he returned to a house on Jasper Street in Rome where his wife and children, ranging in age from a baby to the oldest at seventeen years old were living. He was known to visit Frankfort periodically and it was because of one of those trips that authorities were given a reason to charge him with another murder that had occurred in Frankfort only three months before his eventual capture. As it turned out, Polizzi's movements were being watched closely for several weeks. By monitoring bank deposits made by Polizzi's wife in Rome, detectives were able to pinpoint the location of the Polizzi family and on May 3, 1921, after Detective Bernabic had been upstate for three weeks, he and Herkimer County Deputy Sheriff Herbert led a team of Rome and State Police in capturing the fugitive of nine years. In Polizzi's house were found three revolvers, two of which were loaded, one an automatic, two stilettos and over one hundred rounds of ammunition.

Salvatore Polizzi, offering little resistance, was cooperative and resigned to finally going to trial. He was taken to Frankfort and grilled for hours, a traditional way detectives obtained confessions in that era. Saying he was hungry and needed sleep, he readily admitted to killing John Agietto in 1912. But he insisted that it was an act of self defense after Agietto attacked him with a lethal weapon and he felt his life was in danger. He also said he now had an understanding of how the justice system worked in America and was ready to be tried. With the admission that he was the man who took Agietto's life, he was now grilled about a recent murder in the West Shore Railroad yard in Frankfort, several hundred feet from the spot where John Agietto fell to the ground at Sheldon Avenue and Frankfort Street, nine years earlier.

Albert Dade was a forty-nine-year-old night watchman in the railroad yard. On February 4, 1921, the night foreman of the railroad foundry, John O'Rourke, was walking along the tracks and stumbled across the body of Dade. The watchman had been shot once in the heart with a thirty-eight caliber bullet. For three months it looked as though this would be yet another unsolved crime. But detectives fired up news reporters, making statements that they would soon pin this crime on Salvatore Polizzi, a man already confessing to a Frankfort murder.

Indeed, newspapers published statements given them by police indicating a solid case against the man being called "two gun Sam" and he was now labeled the "alleged killer of Albert Dade". Detectives issued an opinion that they would be grilling Polizzi again and should soon have a confession to both murders if not also the murders of persons in California and Connecticut. Sam was having none of that, however and while admitting he shot Agietto in self defense, flatly denied any knowledge of the Dade shooting.

Frankfort Police Chief Frank Perry was closest to Albert Dade's past history and after quizzing railroad employees about what may have led to such a terrible event, he put together a story of circumstantial evidence that left both the news media and district attorney anxious to pin the Dade murder on Polizzi, who was then charged with both murders and scheduled to go before the grand jury for the Dade crime. He had already been indicted nine years earlier as the Agietto shooter. The assumption that Polizzi killed Albert Dade was based upon one incident involving his sister and brother-in-law. Railyard watchman Dade possessed a notebook that held the names of those living in proximity to the coal piles and coal cars whom he suspected may have been stealing coal. With that information, eight residents living in the

Sheldon Avenue area were taken into custody and interrogated about the Dade murder. Of those questioned, only two were arrested and taken to the Herkimer County Jail. The man and woman arrested were Salvatore Polizzi's brother-in-law and sister. They were arrested for possessing unlicensed weapons and possession of stolen property. It was revealed later that the New York City detective, Michael Bernabic, who spoke Italian, had posed as an umbrella mender, going house to house along Sheldon Avenue, gaining the trust of the neighborhood, even being invited in to share a meal by some. The normally close-lipped immigrants discussed matters in the Dade case that they would never have shared with Police Chief Perry.

An event disclosed by a railroad employee involved the arrested relatives and led to speculation that Polizzi killed watchman Dade, led to his arrest on that charge, making the press confident he would be convicted easily. The day before the shooting it was known that Sam was in town to attend a christening for his sister's baby. The family gathering took place only days after his sister was confronted by watchman Dade. He had grabbed her by the arm and accused her of stealing coal from his employer, the West Shore Railroad. He did release his grip once he saw she was in a delicate condition as a new mother, but his warning was threatening.

In the mind of the press, that was it. "Two gun Sam" was in town and learned what Dade had done to his sister. He killed a man in Frankfort, Connecticut and California. He must have killed Albert Dade. He was convicted in the press, the powerful media of the day, and would sit in the Herkimer County Jail until his trial could be scheduled following the conclusion of another important murder case. The revolvers found in his Rome home were all thirty-eight caliber and Dade was killed with that size pistol. Of course, the technology didn't exist at the time to match the bullet that killed Albert Dade with one of three confiscated guns. Sam's sister and brother-in-law posted bail and were released from jail. Sam was confined to the cell that previously held Chester Gillette, a murderer who had received national attention. Polizzi occupied that cell quietly day after day without speaking to anyone.

Within a month of the Rome capture, a confident district attorney presented his case to the grand jury to obtain an indictment, naming Salvatore Polizzi as the killer of Albert Dade. Detective Bernabic was presented as a man who had been active in murder cases for over twenty years, obtaining dozens of murder convictions. He boasted of a 1911 case where he captured six Italian men within five weeks of the murder of a woman in Croton Lake, New York and all six were sent to the electric chair. Statements were made presenting Polizzi in the darkest of ways. It was reported that he had Sicilian friends from coast to coast and that special precautions had to be invoked to prevent his "black hand" gang from gaining access to him and helping him escape. Prosecutors said they believed Polizzi was a dangerous man and every precaution was being taken so that this prisoner would not exercise his thirst for blood on the authorities.

But exposing the jury to all of that hype may have been a poor strategy. Polizzi repeated the same statement he had made over and over. He repeated once again: "I know nothing about Albert Dade's murder." Dressed totally in black with a magnificent black mustache, he looked directly at the jury and smiled. The jury was unanimous in their verdict:

"We deem the evidence insufficient that Salvatore Polizzi killed Albert Dade." No indictment was brought forward and Polizzi was returned to his cell to now await trial for the shooting death of John Agietto. His incarceration extended for months as discouraged prosecutors said their priorities were dictated by other important cases on the docket. Finally, five months had passed and on November 17, 1921, the first degree murder trial for the July 7, 1912 death of John Agietto, began.

On the opening day of the trial, reporters noted that Salvatore Polizzi's face was lighted with a smile and he was groomed for the occasion. His black mustache was trimmed and his clothes neatly pressed. His wife and young child sat with him. The day was taken up with the procedure of qualifying jurors and the defendant became quite bored. A few events broke the monotony of the day. Deputy Sheriff Al Hickox was in charge of the defendant in the courtroom and when a recess was called, Mr. Hickox, almost dosing off, was unaware that Polizzi had left the courtroom as many others had done. A Barney Fife moment occurred as Hickox jumped to his feet, realizing his charge was no longer with him and began a search for the mustached man. He entered a room in the rear of the courthouse and there sat Sam, feet up on a table, lounged back and smoking a cigar.

During another recess, Sam was very vocal with the famous New York City Detective, Mike Bernabic and Deputy Sheriff Fred Herbert. Both men had been in Rome plotting the capture for three weeks before springing their trap. They were proud of the secretive nature of their investigation and seemed unamused when Polizzi remarked that he was aware of the attention given him and had seen them several times during their visit to the City of Rome. Finally, the jury pool was secured and the next day the actual trial began. In the end, the jury consisted mostly of farmers or residents of many small communities scattered through the county.

Supreme Court Judge Claude Alverson traveled from Watertown to oversee the first degree murder trial. District Attorney W. Earl Ward and his assistant, James H. Green represented the People and Charles D. Thomas and Charles B. Hane, the defendant. The prosecution brought in witnesses, who in the opinion of many observers, scored for the defense. Elia Caruso testified that he attempted to get John Agietto to go into the Caruso house, but claimed Agietto would have no part of that, saying he "was not done with Polizzi." Testimony from several witnesses called by the prosecution was not allowed by Judge Alverson as was the dying man's statements to the doctors. Joseph Agietto, the brother who was playing the guitar and argued with Polizzi at the party, had moved to the French protectorate of Tunisia in Northern Africa before the trial began. Prosecutors were allowed to advance speculation that Polizzi could be a member of a Black Hand or Mafia by tying him in with connections in large cities in different parts of the country.

The defense team attempted to have Doctors Albones, Hayes and Richards conclude that Agietto died of pneumonia he contracted after being shot in both lungs, not the actual wounds to the lungs. But the doctors were unanimous in their opinions that the patient died of "traumatic pneumonia" caused by the bullet wounds. The discussion went back and forth, but in the end it was the gun shots that caused Agietto's death within three days, a shooting that from the day of his capture, Polizzi had admitted committing, a shooting that he claimed was necessary to protect his own life. Over several days, the events that led to the shooting were established by many witnesses and the story as told in the beginning of this chapter was verified by both sides.

Finally, after days of testimony, Salvatore Polizzi took the stand on his own behalf. He described the events leading up to the shooting, which by now, everyone in the courtroom was quite familiar with. His story did not vary from its original nature and his outright admission that he shot John Agietto was once again confirmed. Then, as he approached the point in his description of what transpired before he drew his gun, he demonstrated how he was carrying a coat over his left shoulder with his left hand upright, holding on to the coat. He said his arm was in that position when Agietto plunged a stiletto into his arm and caused him to fear for his life. With no objection by the prosecution, he visited each member of the jury and showed them his left arm, exhibiting an obvious scar, four inches above his wrist and claimed it had been there for nine years following John Agietto's attack on him.

At the conclusion of the case, Attorney Thomas used four hours in his plea for the defense, urging the jury to return a decision of justifiable homicide. He emphatically expressed the defense team's belief that Salvatore Polizzi was well within his rights as allowed by law for the taking of a life. He stated

"If, after Polizzi shot Agietto, he had gone to any lawyer, he would have been told he had nothing to fear, but he did not know the law." The prosecution raised an objection to that statement but was overruled by the court. District Attorney Ward, in a two hour argument to the jury, repeatedly urged conviction for murder in the first degree. Justice Alverson used one and a half hours to charge the jury, warning that a verdict of guilty would result in sending the husband and father to the electric chair. The jury deliberated for four hours before they informed the officer in charge that they had reached a unanimous decision. They returned the verdict requested by the defense. Foreman Chester A. Fort reported "justifiable homicide" to Justice Alverson to which the judge answered "You mean then that you find the accused not guilty," and the reply was "yes." Polizzi was all smiles as he thanked the court and reached out to each juror, thanking them individually.

Absolved of any question of guilt in two Frankfort murders, and never proven to be involved in murder cases in other states, Salvatore Polizzi, a.k.a. "two gun Sam" rejoined his family in Rome. In June 1922 his seventeen-year-old son, Joseph, died at home from tuberculosis. In August, Sam once again made the newspapers when Rome police raided 213 South James Street and charged Salvatore Polizzi with "conducting a gambling joint." A table was covered with money and as officers attempted to seize the cash, many of the bills were torn when reluctant participants attempted to hold on to their part of the pot. Several bottles of illegal liquor were seized as was one revolver. Five players of Ziginette, the Italian poker game, were arrested. Sam settled the matter, pleading guilty to an alcohol charge and soon returned to the village where he originally started by moving back to Frankfort. He had no further weapons violations from that time on. But on May 11, 1923, he was once again the victim of an attack. He was returning from the market, and while entering the front door of his house at 210 Orchard Street, he was hit by the charge from a shotgun blast. Doctors Kelly and Sheffield were called and had him taken by ambulance to the Ilion Hospital. Shot was lodged in his back but not deep enough to cause major damage and he fully recovered. The shooter was apparently waiting for Sam, hiding in an open freight car on a rail siding near the rail station which was directly across the street from Polizzi's home. Sheriff Firth speculated that the act was one seeking vengeance and related to Polizzi's acquittal in the Agietto trial. No one was ever charged with the shooting.

In 1931, Polizzi went to trial after a car salesman claimed he was struck in the face and head by Sam in an altercation over the sale of a car. At a session of Justice Court in the Frankfort Town Hall, presided over by Justice W. H. Waterbury, a jury found him not guilty of assault, third degree. In his later years he was still on probation stemming from weapon charges and in 1940 he was found in violation of his probation terms after an arrest in an alcohol tax case. For that violation he served three months in the Oneida County Jail.

Chapter 8

A Tangled Web of 3 Murders
1919 – 1921

Of three murders committed during a fourteen month period from November 1919 thru February 1921, only one was solved, but some victims and material witnesses in each case had a connection with those involved in one of the other murders. Twenty-seven-year-old Clarence D. Kelley's battered body was found west of Frankfort near the West Shore Railroad tracks on November 28, 1919. Coroner Dr. Ralph Huyck performed the autopsy and ruled that Mr. Kelley had fallen from a train and died due to a fractured skull. The determination of Dr. Huyck that an accidental death had occurred would no doubt been final if not for the belief of the dead man's two brothers who suspected that their brother had been murdered. Though they lived near Buffalo, George and Edward Kelley traveled to Herkimer County and even brought with them, John Doyle, a well known Rochester, N.Y. detective. The threesome influenced the county district attorney and sheriff to pursue their theory that Clarence was robbed and murdered. They contacted a congressman who persuaded the governor to urge a renewed investigation into the matter. The coroner agreed to investigate further and county authorities began searching for new clues that might point to the probability that a murder had taken place. Dr. Huyck issued a modified opinion saying that the skull fracture resulted from a blow which split the scalp from the back of the head at the top to the right ear, causing death and could have resulted only from an assault with an ax, sledge hammer or similar heavy weapon, or by the body falling or being thrown from a rapidly moving vehicle. Nothing was revealed at the autopsy which in any way weakened the theory that Kelley was murdered, but nothing was found that could be used to prove conclusively that murder had been committed.

With increased publicity about the case, and the brothers now offering a one thousand dollar reward, people began coming forward with information. The coroner noted that a deep gash was located on the back of one of the hands of the dead man and Detective Doyle immediately offered a theory that the wound was suffered when Kelley shielded his head to ward off the blow from the heavy object that caused his death. A woman came forward saying she observed an automobile that stopped on the highway near the area where the body was found on the day presumed to be the date Kelley died. She claimed a man was looking over a fence opposite the place where the body was discovered just a few hours later. That fence contained blood stains and scratches indicating a struggle had occurred in that area.

The Kelley brothers were certain that robbery was the motive behind the murder of their brother and that his body was thrown near the railroad tracks, making it look like he had been hit by a train. They informed Herkimer County authorities that Clarence always carried a substantial amount of money on his person as well as a diamond ring and diamond pin, none of which was found with the body. The brothers found a bankbook showing that Clarence was making regular deposits and had a considerable amount of money saved. But the task to find a killer was daunting and because a firearm was not used, the investigation went nowhere.

Clarence Kelley had been in Frankfort the night before he died but a positive identification was not made for three days. One card in a pocket with the initials C.D.K. was the only thing found that helped identify the victim. Once his identity was revealed, records were found that he had applied for and was issued a permit to carry a revolver, based on his statement that he had a lucky escape from an unknown person that had shot at him. He was a salesman and known to carry money on his person at all times. Kelley was living in Herkimer, boarding at the home of Edward Platt. Platt also rented rooms to others and another boarder, Rutger Warder, was acquainted with Kelley.

He was questioned and his room searched. He held a quantity of chair casters, a product that Kelley sold, but said that Kelley had given them to him. He gave detectives the name of another man that had also been given casters. He admitted that he had been in Kelley's room several times as a guest and further admitted that Kelley had shown him his revolver. Even though he had been seen together with Kelley on the street just hours before the estimated time of Kelley's demise, Warder was not held. Rutger Warder had been a boyhood buddy of the district attorney and had been a deputy sheriff several years earlier.

Three months went by and nothing relevant presented itself to the investigation of Clarence Kelley's death. George Kelley had returned to his home near Buffalo with little hope that his brother's killer would ever be found. But then, like something emerging from the dark of night, he received a letter from Utica, voicing the complaint of an apparently scorned woman who claimed her husband was involved in the death of Clarence Kelley. That letter offered little detail but was followed by another one a week later that could be traced to 308 Spring Street in Utica. The Kelley brothers were ecstatic, feeling that their assumption that Clarence was a murder victim would finally be accepted.

Detective Doyle was again engaged by the Kelley family and after a four month investigation that included Deputy Sheriff Ralph Cress, a group of officers descended upon the house they had been watching and searched for a woman named Mrs. Marie Newble, the supposed letter writer. They were informed that she was not home, but a forced search found her hiding in a small building behind the home. She was arrested as a material witness and taken to the Herkimer County Jail. After hours of intense questioning, surrounded by officers including District Attorney Ward, the shaken woman broke down, sprang from her chair and hysterically cried out "My husband is the guilty one."

She claimed her husband was not living with her. He lived in Clinton, N.Y. and the separated wife gave her questioners his address. He was located, returned to Herkimer, charged with first degree murder and incarcerated before midnight. William Newble was fifty years old and employed at the Savage Arms Co., just down the road from the murder scene.

The Newbles had formerly lived in Syracuse and the following day's editions of papers in that city proclaimed in bold headlines:

"One of the most remarkable murder cases has been solved." Before any hint of a grand jury indictment, Newble was condemned as the killer even as he proclaimed total innocence. Marie Newble's revelations during her grilling were leaked to the press and if proven true, would certainly send her husband to the electric chair. She described a diamond ring and diamond pin that her husband had possession of after a confrontation with Clarence Kelley.

Events transpired quickly as an indictment for first degree murder was sought by the prosecutor. At the opening of the grand jury trial, Mr. Newble's counsel introduced himself. He was Assemblyman Louis M. Martin of Clinton, chairman of the judiciary committee of the assembly, attorney and a former school teacher. His statement to the court was clear and distinct. "Absolutely this man is one I have always known to trust. I shall stand with him both personally and professionally until he is cleared, as there is no doubt in my mind he will be and that speedily."

As Marie Newble's story of her husband's involvement in the murder was revealed to the jury, Assemblyman Martin began to question the betrayal of her husband. He revealed that she could be called Mrs. Marie Weiss Randall Rainbow Storms Newble. She was alleged to be a bigamist, marrying William Newble after meeting him at Sylvan Beach and while still married to others. In fact, a husband in Syracuse, Elmer Rainbow, had her served with divorce papers after reading that she was held in Herkimer. He had been an Onondoga

County special deputy sheriff and had been searching for her. Counsel Martin also picked apart Marie's story of her husband's involvement in the case. Her story began with the couple picking up Clarence Kelley as a hitchhiker on the road from Frankfort to Utica. Another couple, Fred Hall and Lena Foster, were said to be in the automobile with the Newbles. They offered a flask of whiskey to Kelley and he refused to drink. The men then took Kelley from the car to an area behind a fence near the railroad tracks, but came back without Mr. Kelley. Once home, Newble showed Marie a diamond ring and diamond stick pin and said he had also taken money from the man they had picked up.

Fred Hall and Lena Foster could not be found and the diamond jewelry was never produced. One can imagine the flushed appearance of the prosecutor's face as the defense tore the story apart. Court was adjourned and Marie became a defendant, charged not only with perjury but also bigamy. Detective Doyle returned to Rochester and the Kelleys returned to western New York, again experiencing a failure in finding their brother's murderer. Four hundred people filled the courthouse area to witness the punishment to be handed out to alleged killer William Newble but instead learned that he was the innocent victim of a vindictive wife. Many would return for her arraignment where she totally broke down and admitted the whole story was a fabrication. Mr. Newble claimed he had worked two jobs and built his wife a new home in Clinton but was unable to avoid their separation because of her strange accusations and charges about things he knew nothing about. Within three months she was sent to the Auburn Prison for Women for two to four years.

Albert Dade's Murder, February 5, 1921
Henry Werner's Murder, February 22, 1921

It was less than a year after William Newble's trial concluded, leaving Clarence Kelley's murder unsolved, that newspaper headlines would again describe other Frankfort shootings. Albert Dade's murder, mentioned prominently in the previous chapter because it was thought that Salvatore Polizzi was Dade's killer, also went unsolved. The body of the forty-nine-year-old employee of the West Shore Railroad was found in the railway yard in the dark of night, shot through the heart and without any witnesses coming forward.

When he was thirty, Albert Dade migrated from France where he had been trained as a machinist. He grew up in a very large family and some of his siblings joined him in America. A brother, John, came to Frankfort. His new country presented all types of opportunities to the ambitious young man and he took full advantage of them. He and his wife purchased a building on Litchfield Street and lived in the upstairs apartment. They operated a confectionery store on the ground floor while he was also employed by the Pratt Chuck Company as a machinist, later moving on to the same position at Remington Typewriter and Savage Arms. He bought a farm near the end of the Frankfort Gorge as an investment and rented it out, then later selling it. Albert was an inventor and although he never patented any of his ideas, his friends admired his unique designs for a beer cooler that worked without using ice, a toy bank and a potato digger.

Dade began working for the railroad, a second job, on the night shift, working with the "ice house gang." That was a group of men packing ice in railroad cars containing meat. Theft was always a worry of management and Albert was hired as a security guard. He would have no part of the rumored practice of some employees sneaking out a few samples of meat. His stern, uncompromising attitude cost him any social interaction with the gang and he soon became despised by several crew members. Things became tense and management thought it best that he work alone as a yard detective, walking a set route in the railyard at night. That was fine with Dade as long as he was allowed to bring his dog, Jack, along with him on his rounds.

Mr. Dade began his rounds in darkness, carrying a gun with him that only he knew was a toy. When a friend found out he didn't have a real gun, he was advised to purchase a real gun. He responded by saying that he could physically handle any situation he would encounter in the yard. And it wasn't long before he encountered a known gang of young "Italian" men carrying bags in which they placed stolen coal, taken from the railroad's bins. Most homes in the area around the railroad yard were heated with coal and wood. By showing his toy gun and urging Jack to chase them, he was able to make them drop their spoils and run away. Jack responded by snatching and ripping the seat out of one of the culprit's pants. Within a few days, Jack came up missing and was never found. This was one month before Albert Dade's murder and the event was one reason that a whole group of "Italians" on Sheldon Avenue were taken into custody after the murder. An incident involving Salvatore Polizzi's sister was the reason for his being charged.

Albert Dade's murder excited the community and the entire area surrounding Frankfort. His wife was devastated and daughter Lucie deeply affected. The response from law enforcement was rapid. Chief of Police Frank Perry, Frankfort Officer Williams, Sheriff Ralph Cress, District Attorney Earl Ward and West Shore Railroad Detectives James Petrel and James Landers became involved immediately. When money was found in the victim's pockets, a motive of robbery was ruled out and the investigation focused on anyone that might have wanted the night watchman silenced.

Members of the ice house gang, several Italian residents who lived along Sheldon Avenue near the coal storage bins and one Polish man who had threatened Albert, were all rounded up and interrogated. Silence was consentaneous, no one knew anything about what happened. A worker, estimated to be three hundred feet from the scene, claimed he never heard a gunshot. Three residents living at Sheldon Avenue were found to have revolvers and arrested on that charge, but could not be tied to the murder. Names of those under suspicion were taken from a notebook Dade kept. It contained a list of those he suspected or had warned about stealing coal. Anton Musovsky, a Polish immigrant known to have threatened Dade, was questioned but later released. His involvement stemmed from the purchase of Dade's farm and then losing it back to Dade when he failed to live up to his end of the bargain. The Supreme Court had awarded the farm back to Dade and after that, Anton had made a threat that he would "get him." Musovsky was well known by authorities, having dealt with him previously when he was involved in an incident with neighbors near the farm. He had used a firearm and shot at a group of "Italians."

Months went by without a clue as to who could have shot Dade in the middle of the night in that lonely railroad yard. Authorities successfully captured Dade suspect Salvatore Polizzi in Rome, New York on May 3rd, but as described in the previous chapter, after examining the evidence presented by the district attorney, a jury failed to indict him for Albert Dade's murder. Then another sensational murder occurred less than three weeks after Dade's body was discovered. The new case shifted most of the district attorney's resources to proving the guilt of a man, a woman and her mother in the shooting death of Henry Werner, while also investigating possible ties to both the Kelley and Dade murders.

The Woodbridge family had been living in Frankfort even before the village was incorporated. Thomas Woodbridge was hired to work in the West Shore Railroad's roundhouse when it first opened for repair work. From there he was trained to be a locomotive fireman and began traveling with passenger trains. His father had been killed in the Civil War. Thomas was hailed as a hero and was said to have saved the lives of several passengers when he jumped from his locomotive and flagged down a train that eventually collided with his. He married a woman from Frankfort, Minnie Lane. They had two daughters and raised them on Mill Street near land that eventually was taken over by feed mill operator, George Corrado. The February 22, 1921 murder case of Henry Werner involved both Minnie and her daughter Jennie Werner, wife of the murdered man.

Henry Werner and Jennie had been married for eleven years when his body was found in a wooded ravine several hundred feet behind their home on the Old Forge Road just outside of Ilion. They had moved from Frankfort four years earlier. On the previous evening, Henry had gone rabbit hunting on the snow under a moon-lit sky. He had been successful that day earlier when he was accompanied by a man who rented a room in the Werner home, Rutger Warder. This was the same man who had previously boarded in a house in Herkimer with Clarence Kelley, the man found murdered in Frankfort. In that case, described earlier in this chapter, Warder was questioned but never charged.

When Henry Werner failed to return home from hunting that night, Jennie contacted her husband's father, Lucius Werner, who lived nearby. Henry had stayed overnight at his parents home in the past and she said she had assumed he was there. But the elder Werner said that his son never came to his house and was worried because he had heard a shot during the evening. Fearing an accidental shooting, he went looking for his son, but couldn't find him. Several hours later, a young neighbor named Ralph Harter was running a dog to hunt rabbits when his hound started howling at the top of a ravine and brought him to Henry's body. Harter recognized his neighbor and saw that he had been shot in the head and was dead. Ralph ran to a home that had a telephone and the sheriff and coroner were called. Upon returning to the body, he observed Rutger Warder near the body.

Sheriff Cress, District Attorney Ward and Coroner Manion examined the body and at first the coroner leaned toward announcing that a suicide or hunting accident was the cause of Henry's death. But Sheriff Cress' mind was processing in a Sherlock Holmes manner after he discovered who the boarder was in the Werner home. He immediately told the district attorney that he suspected foul play. Sheriff Cress had always suspected that Rutger Warder, the man now renting a room from the dead man, was the killer of Clarence Kelley. Mr. Warder was once again living in a house with another murder victim. When it was found that a double barreled shotgun with both chambers loaded but not discharged lay next to the body, it solidified the sheriff's thinking. This was no suicide and the truncated distance between the shooter and Henry, as determined by the amount of injury to the victim's head, ruled out an accidental shot from another hunter.

Sometimes guilt is obvious and Sheriff Cress' hypothesis fell into place as Rutger Warder's absence from the scene of the shooting during the arrival of authorities and his seemingly having little interest in the affairs of the investigation were perceived by the county officials present as unusual. When it was learned that Warder had accompanied Henry on the previous night's hunting trip, the case against Warder was substantial and Cress wasted no time in arresting him as a material witness, taking him to the Herkimer County Jail for interrogation. At first Warder told Cress that he was present when Henry had sold beef to some Italians in Frankfort and Henry got into an altercation with them about money. He claimed they said they would "get him" and he figured they hid in the woods and shot him. But questioning methods were intense in 1921 and after several hours of continuous grilling, Rutger Warder broke down and confessed that he shot Henry Werner in the head with a shotgun.

What happened immediately following his confession had Frankfort and Ilion in a buzz. Jennie Werner and her mother Minnie Woodbridge of Frankfort were taken into custody and also arrested on first degree murder charges. Although it was late at night, they too were grilled with the intention of obtaining confessions. Mother and daughter were implicated in Warder's confession as being fully involved in the plot to kill Henry and what the confessed killer had told investigators was, in their minds, plausible.

Soon it was revealed that living with Henry Werner had become unbearable for Jennie and her six-year-old daughter Elma. Jennie, said to be a very attractive young lady, was described as being a hard working wife and mother who kept a spotless house. But Henry was said to be a drunkard who hung out in the saloons at Frankfort and treated Jennie poorly. Jennie had left Henry twice and said she was sorry she had listened to a judge who advised her to return to him. She claimed that upon returning to Henry a second time, he warned her that if she ever left him again he would kill her.

The confession of Rutger Warder was obtained after he had been shown a confession signed by Jennie. He read the document, but said at first, the signature was not hers. Sheriff Cress convinced him that she was under emotional stress and it was her signature. When Warder finally came clean he blamed Jennie and her mother, Minnie Woodbridge, for planning the death of Henry for several weeks. Rutger Warder was described as a six-foot-tall good looking thirty-year-old man. His life seemed to take no planned path. He was born on the Warder farm in the Town of Russia where he chummed around in his youth with the district attorney he would now face, W. Earl Ward. He moved to Little Falls and worked in a garage as a mechanic. He married and his wife Wanda delivered a daughter, but a year before the murder had obtained a divorce after being separated several years. A Herkimer woman was mentioned in the divorce action. He was involved in an incident while employed as a chauffeur for the wealthy Marks family in Herkimer. He reported that while in the family's garage, a sensational attack on him had taken place, claiming an unknown man had beaten him unconscious. The attacker was never found. In Herkimer, when he boarded at the Platt house he was acquainted with murder victim Clarence Kelley who also lived there. Warder became a friend of Henry Werner and when he agreed to work with Henry, buying cattle from the farms surrounding the valley, Henry agreed to rent Rutger Warder a room in his home. Another fact revealed about the murdered man was that he was a good friend of Albert Dade whose unsolved murder took place seventeen days before Henry was killed and at one point, detectives thought Werner was killed to silence his knowledge about the Dade homicide.

The first of the three persons who went to trial, charged with first degree murder, was Rutger Warder on March 22nd. His defense was based upon his confession implicating Jennie Werner and her mother Minnie Woodbridge. If he were to be believed, the plot to kill Henry was hatched in the Mill Street home of Minnie Woodbridge in Frankfort and the "doing away" of Jennie's husband was planned for months. Rutger and Jennie had been seen visiting the Woodbridge home.

The alleged killer's statements led to the arrest of Minnie and her daughter. Rutger described planning that started early in the fall of 1920, months before the crime. He claimed that shortly after he moved in with the Werners, Jennie told him she hated her husband and wished he were dead. He said Jennie told him that she was in love with him and they had to get rid of her husband. Several times, plans were devised by Jennie and her mother. Warder took a revolver with him on a fishing trip with which he was supposed to shoot Henry, but he lost his nerve. On other hunting trips he again failed to carry through with the plan and another time when Henry was very drunk, Warder carried him to bed and Jennie told him to go to the drugstore and obtain poison. But Warder said he told her the drugstore was closed. He claimed she began to accuse him of cowardice. He described a plan devised by Minnie Woodbridge where she as a nurse could obtain poisonous wood alcohol. Warder could mix it with whiskey that Henry would drink. He made a statement that "It was for her and for the love of her that I did this deed."

On April 9th at 2 a.m., after nine hours of deliberation, the jury returned a verdict that Rutger Warder had committed first degree murder. Dozens of friends and relatives cried and let their emotions flow as the district attorney had advanced his boyhood idol (Warder was the star player of his high school baseball team) to a death sentence. He was sent to the Sing Sing Prison death house to be executed during the week of May 16. But once he was incarcerated, he turned on Jennie and told officials he had lied to shift blame for the actual crime from Jennie and her mother. He claimed she was the one who actually killed her husband by hitting him on the head with an ax in the cellar of their home and that he had held Henry's body while she discharged the contents of a double barrel shotgun into her husband's head, destroying evidence of the ax wound. He claimed he reloaded both barrels of the gun and placed it by the body, unwittingly eliminating a possible suicide verdict. He also claimed that he took the body to the ravine in the woods where it was found the next morning. He described further planning by Jennie to escape detection. He was to go to Frankfort, visit with her mother, then return and help Henry's father look for the missing hunter. He said she put hot pepper in Warder's shoes to throw off a scent if bloodhounds were used to track the killer and burned the shoes in the furnace when Warder returned from dumping the body. Parts of his new confession had verification. The sheriff's team did discover shoe eyelets in the furnace ashes and found blood stains on the basement floor and furnace itself. But Jennie claimed Henry butchered animals in the cellar on different occasions. Details of Warder's story, once he was facing the electric chair in a few weeks, gave his boyhood pal, District Attorney W. Earl Ward confidence to continue the first degree murder charges against Jennie Werner and her mother Minnie Woodbridge and Jennie's trial began on April 18, 1921. Minnie would be tried separately.

Rutger Warder was brought from Sing Sing Prison to once again testify that Jennie had killed her husband with an ax and that her mother was involved in planning her son-in-law's demise. The prosecution questioned Henry Werner's father for over two hours and had him repeat a statement he made previously that Jennie came to him after the body was found and said "I hope you will forgive me for what I have done." The trial drew huge crowds and hundreds of people were called to be jurors. The initial trial of Rutger Warder and now the trial of Jennie bankrupted the county court fund. A special meeting had to be called by the Board of Supervisors to find funding to continue with the court procedure. The defense attacked confessions made by Jennie after her arraignment immediately following the discovery of her husband's body, saying she was under extreme duress and had made admissions that she had no understanding of.

During the two week trial, the methodology used by the prosecution and defense teams became clear. Prosecutors brought Rutger Warder out of Sing Sing to testify that it was Jennie and her mother that wanted Henry done away with and in Warder's newest version of how Henry was killed, Jennie swung the ax that hit Henry in the head in the basement of their home after she and her mother had planned but never carried through with plans to poison him. A life insurance policy payable to Jennie was read in full during the proceedings and details of a bad relationship leading to separations was presented to the jury.

The defense team had plenty of ammunition. They threw an idea before the court that Rutger Warder had not only killed Henry, but a year earlier had killed Clarence Kelley, the man he lived with in Herkimer. George Kelley, the murdered man's brother was put on the stand and testified that a pocketbook found by police in Warder's trunk was indeed his brother's. With that charge they implied that Henry Werner may have had knowledge of his friend Albert Dade's murder and the Kelley Murder. Was Rutger Warder a serial killer that duped the Werner household? The defense was eager to present Dr. Albert H. Hamilton from Auburn, N.Y., a noted expert who had previously testified in one hundred and forty murder trials. He had examined the basement where Warder claimed Jennie had first shot Henry and the spot in the ravine where the body was found. Dr. Hamilton gave testimony that the cellar could not have been the scene of a struggle and killing and that Warder could not have, alone, carried Henry's body to the spot in the woods where it was found. He tested the traces of blood found in the basement and made the same conclusion that Little Falls chemist Dr. John Hurley had; the blood was not of human origin. His opinion was that Henry had been killed with a single shot shotgun, not the double barrel gun found by the body that Warder said Jennie used to cover up the ax wound. The defense brought in friends claiming the Werner's marriage was not as bad as described and that the two separations were caused solely by Henry's excessive drinking. Finally, Jennie's lawyers had her take the stand. She denied any relationship with Rutger Warder and she firmly denied all claims that portrayed her as an accomplice, ending with recall of Rutger Warder's first words to her as he came from the woods the night of the murder:

"I've done it." Jennie: "You've done what?"

"I've killed Henry. If you tell on me, I'll lay it on you."

Before Jennie's case was handed to the jury, the defense called a friend of Rutger Warder to the stand who testified that during a visit to Warder's jail cell on the first day of his incarceration, Warder told him, "I done it, now I'm going to pay." And, indeed, he was sent to the electric chair by the jury. Would Jennie Werner suffer the same fate?

On May 11th, the case was delivered to the jury at 6:30 p.m. and throughout the night, streets around the courthouse overflowed with those anxious to hear the verdict. They had a long wait. At 7:00 a.m. word was finally received that Jennie had been found "not guilty." The widow that had been incarcerated for almost three months was free to return to raise her child. But her mother was still facing a trial for the same charge, first degree murder and Rutger Warder was still scheduled to be electrocuted within a few weeks.

Rutger Warder's sentence of death by electric chair was appealed and proceedings successfully delayed that event for another twenty months until Governor Al Smith commuted his sentence to life imprisonment. The governor's action came after a hearing was held in Albany at which the parents of the slain man, Mr. And Mrs. Linus Werner appeared and added their pleas for clemency to those of Warder's council. His council claimed that throughout Herkimer County the opinion of residents was that Warder should not go to the electric chair and that most residents of the community in which the crime was committed seriously doubted Warder's alleged part in the actual killing.

Petitions, signed by many of Warder's neighbors and almost all residents of the immediate vicinity, the council contended, were presented to the governor at the hearing. The most notable fact about those petitions was that among the signers were the members of the jury that determined the verdict. Warder's attorneys claimed the conviction was based largely upon a confession he made after his arrest, but which was repudiated during the trial and before his conviction.

In announcing his decision, Governor Smith said:

"I have no doubt about the guilt of Warder, but I have doubt about the justice of exacting him from the full penalty of the law. While it is true that his first confession was supported by certain circumstantial evidence, it is also true that future developments may indicate other people involved as seriously, if not so more than Warder himself." At Sing Sing Prison, Rutger became a chauffeur to the prison's famous warden, Lewis E. Lawes and was eventually released on parole.

Further developments as described by Governor Smith did not occur and Jennie returned to the Mill Street homestead in Frankfort, living there for many decades. She married Leroy Hills and then later moved to Binghamton, N.Y. where she died in 1981 at the age of ninety-one. Her mother, Minnie Woodbridge spent three more weeks in jail before District Attorney Ward agreed to her release on June 2nd. A not guilty verdict determination of her daughter's trial gave the prosecution little hope of ever convicting the mother of planning and abetting the murder. She returned to Frankfort and eight years later married Frank Falsen, a man who had originally come to Frankfort from Oslo, Norway. He ran a furniture store on Main Street for many years. Minnie died in 1961 at the age of ninety-four.

Chapter 9

Murder in a Strawberry Patch 1924

This is a sad story about one young man's life being cut short and the lives of a young immigrant and his family being changed forever by a shooting that happened in an instant, in a strawberry patch. Stanislaus Kurkowski and his brother were born in Poland but migrated to America and settled in Utica. Another brother chose to relocate in Pennsylvania. Stanley, as he would now be known, was an industrious young man and married a girl from Utica. They began a family and in 1924 when Stanley was thirty-one, had three children, ages eight, five and eighteen months. During the same time period, Carlo LaBardo, three years older than Stanley, came to the Village of Frankfort from Italy. He too was an industrious young man and was soon able to purchase a house on Orchard Street in 1922, while he and his wife raised a large family that included five children. Only a few years after he moved into the Orchard Street home he heard that Antonio Loiacano was selling a small farm on the Utica–Frankfort Road near Stop 4 on the trolley line. With the kids growing up, Charles (as he was now called) saw a golden opportunity in the extensive strawberry fields that had been planted and cultivated by his friend "Toni" Loiacano. What encouraged him to buy the farm was Toni's offer to hold the mortgage. Toni had bought the farm fourteen years previous. So before strawberry season arrived in 1924, Charles and his family had moved to the farm after selling the Orchard Street home in the village.

When strawberry picking began, Charles soon discovered a disadvantage in the way the farm was arranged. The berry patch was not visible from the farmhouse but it was easily accessible from the busy highway leading to Utica. It was later reported by Charles Cooper, a neighbor on the next farm, that as many as five crates of berries had been stolen from Charles LaBardo's patch and neighboring berry patches before a life-changing incident occurred at Charles' patch. On July 10th, nearing the end of strawberry picking season, Polish immigrant Stanley Kurkowski parked his Ford truck near the side of the road adjoining Charles' berry patch. He had asked the friends riding with him to join him in enjoying a few strawberries and they obliged. The group walked into the rows of berry plants, picking and eating at will. They unwittingly walked into what turned out to be a very dangerous situation.

Charles, now a farmer out in the country, had armed himself with a double barrel shotgun to deal with any unforeseen threats to his family and was guarding his fruit with the gun. He spotted the group of strangers in his field and grabbed his weapon to chase off the intruders. With his limited ability of the English language he gave out a warning to those in his berries. Everyone ran back to the truck, parked out of site from the picking area, except Stanley Kurkowski. With his equal lack of proficiency in English, he attempted to deal with the angry man carrying the shotgun. Those at the truck heard one shot and the fear of being shot lead them to head for Utica.

Neighbor Charles Cooper heard the shotgun blast and ran to investigate. He discovered a severely injured Stanley Kurkowski who had attempted to get back to the road, but had collapsed and was in agony. He had been shot in the chest and was bleeding badly. Another neighbor contacted Frankfort Doctor Brian J. Kelly. Upon his arrival, Frankfort's most popular doctor knew immediately he had to get the shooting victim to the Ilion hospital. At the hospital it was determined that three ribs and a lung had been destroyed. Dr. Kelly did what he could but offered little hope of recovery. He summoned Dr. Sheffield from Frankfort. He was the coroner and took an antemortem statement from Stanley while the dying man was visited by his brother, wife and three children. He died the next afternoon but not before he was able to tell the coroner and district attorney that yes, he had been stealing strawberries, but had offered to pay for them before being shot by an angry man who would not listen to him. He was unable to tell who the man was or where the shooter had gone following the blast.

Stanley's companions returned and were unable to tell police what happened; they had only heard the shot. Law-enforcement first upon the scene, Officer Fisher of the Frankfort Police and Herkimer County Sheriff Firth went to the farm and made a complete search of the property. There they found Charles' wife and children, but no one had any information on the whereabouts of their husband and father. The shotgun used was found hidden in a barrel of trash in the barn. Once the manhunt was publicized, Utica Police received a report from a man who claimed he knew the fugitive and had seen him driving his truck in the city. An intensive search was conducted in the Broad Street area but nothing was found. It was later determined that Charles' truck had been left with Antoni Loiacano, the man who held the mortgage on the farm. When the Rome, New York Police Department became involved in the case, the *Rome Sentinel* newspaper ran with a story claiming a cold blooded murder had occurred in Frankfort, saying it was rumored that Kurkowski had knelt before the farm owner, kissing his hand and begging him not to shoot him. Of course, no one had witnessed such an event.

Papers were now giving the shooter's name as Charles Ribardo, not LaBardo, and that did turn out to be correct. An unfruitful search for Ribardo went on for months. On August 12th a sale of property was held by the Sheriff as ordered by Supreme Court Justice Devendorf to pay off debts left by the missing man. Six cows, a team of horses and a group of farm implements and articles were sold. Charles Ribardo's dream of a family farm was over. James Smithson's claim for animal feed supplied and Antoni Loiacano's notes held were now paid. Mrs. Ribardo and her five children moved back to Frankfort and stayed with friends. And that was it, Charles Ribardo was gone and the authorities had no leads. Looking back, there was an obvious lead in the case when Mrs. Ribardo and her children left Frankfort. Apparently no detective took an interest in that occurrence.

Four months after the shooting, the November session of

the Herkimer County Grand Jury met and indicted a still missing Charles Ribardo on a first degree manslaughter charge. Meanwhile, in the Village of Frankfort there were many rumors, but no one would admit they knew where the Ribardo family went and the close-lipped Italian community remained silent for seventeen years until a tip was received by those still working on the case. An anonymous tip claimed that the Ribardos, including Mr. Ribardo had been living in Brooklyn, New York the entire time since the year of the shooting.

New York City Detective Frank Varrelman arrested and booked a fifty-two-year-old male named Charles Ribardo as the fugitive suspect in the slaying of Stanley Kurkowski seventeen years previous. He contacted Herkimer County Sheriff Charles Madison and the Sheriff, along with New York State Trooper Louis Johnson went to Brooklyn and brought the prisoner back to Herkimer, where he was arraigned on the original indictment of first-degree manslaughter by County Judge Frank Shall. By the time Ribardo was caught, District Attorney Ward and Sheriff Firth, who presented the case to the grand jury originally, were both deceased. Many residents did not even remember the case. Newspapers presented a large photo of Charles Ribardo in handcuffs between Sheriff Madison and Trooper Johnson with an accompanying story of what happened so long ago. A trial had been scheduled to take place in September, two months away.

But Judge Shall, after conferring with Ribardo's attorney James P. O'Donnell, agreed to setting bail at seventy-five hundred dollars, the equivalent of one hundred and twenty thousand dollars today. Bail was posted by Peter and Josephine Caiola and Joseph and Antoinette Loiacano of

Frankfort. Mr. Ribardo pled not guilty and was released. Police released facts about the fugitive's seventeen year hiatus, one of which was that his wife and five children had joined him in Brooklyn, only six months after the shooting and that they had had another child while in Brooklyn.

Before the September trial took place, everyone was surprised that District Attorney Carl W. Peterson allowed Mr. Ribardo to change his plea of not guilty to the first-degree manslaughter charge to guilty of a second-degree charge. Allowing him to accept the lesser charge still meant he could face a maximum of 15 years in prison or a fine of $1000 or both. Mrs. Ribardo and one son attended the trial, as did a son and daughter of the victim, Stanley Kurkowski. Finally, after seventeen years of hiding, Charles seemed ready to accept his fate and be sent to prison, having not understood the language of the judge's ruling making him a free man. He still lacked proficient skills in the English language and only when a group of friends from Frankfort explained the meaning of Judge Shall's suspension of his sentence of three to five years in Attica prison, did he smile.

Those that remembered news coverage at the time of the shooting were stunned. The crime was reported as a cold-blooded shooting, one of Herkimer County's worst. Kurkowski was portrayed as attempting to pay for the berries he and his friends had picked yet was fatally shot while begging for his life. But at the trial, seventeen years later, both the defense and the prosecution basically agreed that the story of the shooting was much different. Both sides agreed upon the court's suspension of a prison sentence, saying testimony would have shown Kurkowski was not shot in cold blood but in a struggle with Ribardo over the latter's shotgun. It was further revealed that Ribardo had borrowed one thousand dollars (sixteen thousand dollars today) from friends in Frankfort and had it paid to Stanley Kurkowski's widow.

Before suspending Mr. Ribardo's sentence, Judge Shall pointed out that he had a letter from the pastor of Ribardo's church in Brooklyn, describing the defendant as a model citizen and active church worker for the past seventeen years. The judge had also received a petition signed by many Frankfort residents including Mayor B.J. Kelly (the doctor who had operated on Kurkowski) and three clergymen, all asking the judge for a suspended sentence. Judge Shall said he approved the settlement made by Ribardo to Kurkowski's widow as preferable to a fine, which would have gone to the state.

In retrospect, what happened in the strawberry patch that day, was sadly the result of each man being unable to properly communicate in a common language and was just one story of many similar happenings during a time when so many emigrated from Europe to a land of great opportunity.

Chapter 10

Another Murder in a Berry Patch
1926

Amazingly, only two years after Stanley Kurkowski was shot and killed in a strawberry patch, an almost identical crime took place just a few miles closer to the Village of Frankfort. But this act appeared to be premeditated first degree murder. The victim, Frank Oliver, and the shooter, Procopico Catalino had become friends after Frank arrived in the village, emigrating from Italy in 1901 at the age of fifteen. At an early age, Frank Oliver was determined to be a merchant in the village. He married Mary Jackson, who was also born in Italy but was brought to Frankfort by her parents when she was only six years old.

Frank did become a young merchant, opening a small grocery store that became well supported by the immigrant community. The success of that small store enabled him to eventually purchase Joseph List's building on West Main St. next to the Baptist Church, the site of List's Furniture Store for many years. Oliver turned it into a fine retail grocery and meat market. He also became a respected wholesaler in the grocery trade. In 1909, at the age of twenty-three he leased

Clarence Fox's building next door and set up a macaroni manufacturing facility, making several hundred pounds of pasta daily. And of course, when prohibition was passed in Washington, and was so unpopular within the immigrant community comprised of those from Ireland, Germany, Poland, Italy and Sicily, the store was just one of many raided by federal agents. Four barrels of Frank's wine was tested by dry officers and contained eleven percent alcohol. The confiscation that followed did not make many in the immigrant community happy.

In 1922 someone ignited the exterior rear portions of both the Oliver and Fox buildings in the early morning hours. Kerosene was splashed on siding and burlap meat bags were ignited, but the blaze was detected early and the fire department contained the fire to the exterior of each building. By 1925, Frank announced that he would be doing an extensive renovation of his business. He sold his home on Orchard Street and purchased the large brick homestead at the corner of West Main and Cemetery Streets. The building was said to be one of Frankfort's oldest landmarks, constructed by one of Frankfort's first doctors, Dr. W.W. Budlong. It was later the home and office of Dr. Parkhurst. The large home was perfect for the grocer's family, which now included four children.

During the same time period when Frank Oliver was building both his family and business, Procopico Catalino, Oliver's Orchard Street neighbor, became good friends with the Olivers. He was ten years older than Frank and his family included seven children. In 1904 he had married Giovanetta (Jennie) Lombardo and once established in Frankfort, he used the first name Michael. Unlike Frank the merchant, Mike Catalino was a laborer, taking whatever job he could find, usually at lower wages and struggling to support his large family. A close friendship developed between the two men, demonstrated when each family added children, as Oliver asked Catalino to be godfather for two of his children and Catalino in turn asked Frank to be godfather for two of his youngest children. Mike had the house on Orchard Street, but took out another mortgage on a small farm on the Mucky Run Road just west of the village. The farm would probably provide him with additional income, but soon he became heavily overextended financially and his friend Frank Oliver became one of his biggest creditors. His obligation increased until he owed hundreds of dollars on his grocery bill.

The farmhouse was empty but Mike was able to work the farm as a fruit and vegetable producer. The bond between the two men ended abruptly when Oliver was forced financially to seek a judgment on Mike's grocery bill. By the time the farm was actually producing fruits, vegetables and berries in 1926, Mike owed Frank six hundred dollars. That amount in today's dollars would be almost eight thousand dollars and Frank couldn't survive in the grocery business for long if he extended that much credit to customers. A judgment was issued by the court and the proceedings spiraled into a situation where Mike Catalino was forced into bankruptcy. He blamed Oliver for all of his troubles as he faced losing both of his properties. The farm was listed as an asset and Oliver, being in the grocery business, told his former friend that he would recover some of his debt by harvesting whatever was available at the farm. A large crop of blackberries was ripening and Oliver could wholesale them at a good profit. But Mike went into a rage when told of Oliver's plan, warning him not to go near the farm and to absolutely stay out of the berry patch. Frank's wife, Mary, was a witness to Mike's threats on more than one occasion and the repeated confrontations caused Frank to visit the Frankfort law firm of Wilbur and Winslow to request a peace bond be placed on Mike. A peace bond is issued to prevent an assault; Oliver felt that threatened.

On Saturday evening, August 21, 1926, Frank's son August, visited Benny Zito's Orchard Street store and poolroom. Mike Catalino showed up and witnesses claimed he told August that his father was a traitor and would soon be dead. Nothing further happened but "Gus" undoubtedly relayed Mike's message to his father.

On the following Thursday, August 26th, the blackberry crop was at its peak and in spite of Mike's threats, Frank chose to go to the farm and pick berries. He hired Louis DiPiazza to work with him and brought his wife and fourteen-year-old son Dominick along to help him. He also brought a thirty-two caliber revolver for protection. The farm was less than a quarter-mile from a work site where the county was installing a new section of roadway on the Mucky Run Road and Mike Catalino had been hired as a laborer. The work crew was under the direction of foreman Bert Randall who at five a.m. that morning had laid-off Mike for the day because it was raining. On the night before, he had instructed Mike not to report to work unless the weather was good but Mike showed up with his raincoat and lunch in hand. Mike went to his empty farmhouse and was never seen again that morning.

The rain let up and Oliver's group of berry pickers arrived at the rows of bushes and spread out to begin harvesting blackberries. Each picker was out of view of the others, hidden by the height of the bushes and the sumac trees that surrounded the berry patch. Louis DiPiazza was picking closest to the road and was within speaking distance of Mrs. Daniel Quail who was sitting in a parked car alongside the road, waiting for her husband to return from his business involving the county road job. She had conversed with Frank Oliver, before he entered the patch.

Only minutes after that conversation, the sharp report of a shotgun blast broke the silence of the morning. DiPiazza jokingly yelled to Mrs. Quayle that someone was going to have rabbit for supper. While he initially didn't suspect foul play, the proximity of the blast caused him to call out to his employer, Frank Oliver. He received no response from Frank but the others in the party did answer. Louis realized he had better seek out his friend and soon came upon Frank, face downward, lying on the ground. Next to him was his thirty-two caliber revolver. Even in the panic of the moment, suicide made no sense.

Louis contacted Dr. W. E. Hayes of Frankfort, but upon his arrival, the doctor found that Frank Oliver was dead; not of a wound from his revolver, but shot at close range with a shotgun by someone facing him. The charge entered Frank's body above the left lung and carried through his back. Frankfort Police Chief Schachel arrived at the scene and immediately summoned the Herkimer County Sheriff's Department to help solve the crime. District Attorney James Green arrived with deputies, Robert Parry and Ray Stanley.

Louis DiPiazza took Mrs. Oliver and her son Dominick from the scene, but not before all parties told the authorities that there had been three weeks of threats directed at Frank Oliver by Mike Catalino. They explained that the farm upon which they were standing belonged to Catalino and the search for the obvious killer began.

Police examined the revolver, and found it was fully loaded and had never been fired. They surmised that Oliver had drawn the gun from his pocket to defend himself, but died before he could use it. They found that the murder victim had almost two hundred dollars in his pockets, ruling out robbery as a motive. Then, in a clump of bushes near the scene of the crime, police found a smoking pipe later identified as belonging to Catalino and when a large posse was organized to search for the missing five-foot-five, stockily-built alleged killer, a loaf of bread wrapped in paper and coat were found. The bread was later identified as probably purchased by Catalino the night before at Michael Ruffalo's Orchard Street market. The coat was identified by a fellow road gang worker, Thomas Castello, as being the property of Mike Catalino. The murder weapon was never found.

Searchers identified tracks in a wet hillside as probably those of a fleeing man fitting Catalino's stature. As word of the crime reached the village, many residents volunteered to participate in the search and it became a massive manhunt. Herkimer County authorities went to the Catalino home on Orchard Street and placed Giovanetta Catalino (Mike's wife) and daughter Anna Gallo under arrest as material witnesses. They were taken to the Herkimer County Jail but were later released when they each posted five thousand dollars bail. A total of four homes in the village were searched "basement to attic" with nothing of importance found. In the Catalino home, shotgun shells, matching the type used in the shooting were found. Catalino's twenty-one-year-old son went missing shortly after the shooting.

The close knit and tight lipped Italian community around Orchard Street was shocked that this tragedy had happened to two families that had been so close in the past. They knew that the man being sought was a godfather to two of the dead man's children and many surmised that Catalino had run off and committed suicide in remorse. And as the woods surrounding the farm were massively searched, the group thought they were simply looking for a body. A tip was received at the police office in Frankfort at midnight and, in spite of the hour, was acted upon immediately. State troopers, sheriff deputies and a new patrolman in the village department, Bob Caivana went to the Laconnti farm in East Winfield. Bob Caivana later became Frankfort Police Chief for many years. After a long ride over terrible roads, they surrounded the farmhouse and demanded admittance to the house. The badly frightened residents at first refused to open the door until assured the group was made up of police officials. When finally admitted and given permission to search the residence, no sign of a fugitive was found and they returned to the village.

Another search south of the village was conducted by walking through wooded areas presumably again looking for the victim of a suicide. Kicking at every suspected object in the underbrush as possibly being a body, a suspicious cache of goods was found, beneath tree branches carefully placed to hide the pile from view. Removal of the covering revealed a pile of merchandise obviously worth thousands of dollars. Tools of all types, paint, rope and wire fencing, all brand new, were many of the items hidden. A wagon trail led to a farmhouse with a truck parked nearby. When the owner of the house was determined, solving the mystery that they had uncovered was easy. The owner, George Polisse, was a car inspector at the Utica railroad yards and every item discovered was identified as stolen from parked railroad cars. He was arrested, taken from his wife and children and placed in the Herkimer County Jail.

The Frankfort Center section of town was adjacent to the murder scene and was thought to be the most likely place Catalino or Catalino's body would be found. Utica City Detectives Thomas Ferrara and Samuel Slade were assigned to the area along with several state troopers, but it was Ferrara's fluency in Italian that was most useful as they searched barns and residences owned by Italian immigrants. Back in the village, Judge Waterbury's chamber was made a command post for the massive search operation. But, one by one, each search group reported back as having little success.

Authorities tried a new tactic, resulting from the lack of success in searching for Catalino's body. It was now felt that he had not committed suicide so they put out a story directed at the Italian community in an attempt to get the shooter to turn himself in if he was still in the area. They wanted to get the word out to Catalino that since Oliver's revolver was found removed from his pocket, Catalino may have a successful reason to plead self-defense on the first degree murder charge.

On Monday, four days after the shooting, Frank Oliver's funeral was held and investigators were still in the village. A group of detectives scoured the northern section of town because word on the street was that Mike Catalino was still somewhere in the village. All vehicles entering or leaving the village were stopped and searched. The day, however, was dedicated to the loss of one of Frankfort's leading merchants. Drapes were drawn in all store windows in respect to their fellow businessman. The funeral procession was led by eight automobiles filled with flowers, followed by the Frankfort Band leading over fifty cars filled with mourners, Mary Oliver and her four children, Julia, August, Dominick and Joseph.

Several days went by and by then the consensus of law enforcement was aligned with public opinion that Mike Catalino had successfully left Central New York. County authorities decided to print posters for distribution throughout the country but were confronted with a problem. They were unable to obtain a picture of the wanted man. After a week went by, they were given a wedding photograph that contained Mike's image. The irony of the situation was that the photograph was one that had Mike and Frank standing side-by-side. They received permission to cut the image of Mike out of the photo to be used on a wanted poster.

More than a month went by and the case looked like it would lie in dormancy unless Mike Catalino was discovered in some faraway venue. But on September 6th, Mary Oliver went to the Herkimer County Sheriff's Office, obviously in a highly emotional state. She described an incident that had occurred at 6 a.m. that morning near her home on West Main Street and was asking for police protection. She claimed her fourteen-year-old son Dominick had seen his father's alleged killer in an alley behind the Oliver residence and that the man covered his face and ran away when discovered. She stated that some in the Italian colony were saying that Procopico (Mike) Catalino had been seen in the village.

Once again, another intensive search took place, and once again, dozens of Italian immigrants were questioned. It was revealed that during the previous week, there were rumors on the street that Procopico had made threats that he intended to kill both Mrs. Oliver and her seventeen-year-old son, August. County and village authorities saturated the area surrounding the widow's home, making a highly visible presence for several days but no sightings of Mr. Catalino were observed.

Many rumors surfaced speculating on the whereabouts of the fugitive; none led to his capture. A few more months passed without any new developments until November 12th when the New Britain, Connecticut Police Department contacted the Herkimer County Sheriff and said they believed a man struck by a train and lying unconscious in a hospital there answered the description supplied by the circular they held at police headquarters. It later proved to be a false identification. In December, the county posted a one thousand dollar reward for information leading to the capture of Mike Catalino. The reward would never be claimed. In April of 1927, Catalino's son-in-law purchased the Catalino home. The grocery business of Frank Oliver was taken over by August Oliver and was renamed Frank Oliver and Son. The large brick home that Frank Oliver had envisioned as a homestead for him and his family was taken over by a Little Falls Bank and ten years after the murder, the building was removed from the corner of West Main Street and Cemetery Street. Years later August Oliver moved the grocery business to the corner of Second Avenue and Reese Road. He became postmaster in Frankfort from 1956 until his death in 1965. Unlike Albert Dade's death five years earlier, where the killer was unknown and the murder remains unsolved, Frank Oliver's killer was identified but never captured.

Chapter 11

Another Farm Murder 1926

John B. Reese, born in Trenton, New York, came to the tiny community of Frankfort in 1837. He and his wife Louisa settled on land adjoining the easterly portion of what is now the village and still is sometimes referred to as the reservation. The flat land was ideal for farming and the Reeses farmed almost two hundred acres. The road running southerly from Main Street to the farm was eventually named Reese Road. It extended to the Joslin farm and Joslin Hill. The Reese's son David took over the farm when John B. died in 1902. Two of his brothers had died at the ages of eleven and twenty-two, leaving him to manage the farm alone. But David and Nancy had a son to carry on the family farm. David Jr. helped his father expand the farm to include greenhouses for growing and selling flowers, shrubs and trees. Poultry buildings were constructed for the production of chickens and eggs. The herd of milk cows was increased to a number where they were able to establish a milk route and expand that business by taking over the Slocum milk route in the village.

But in 1924 a tragedy occurred that impacted both the business and the family forever. David Reese Jr. and Lee Walker had leased the Bargy farm, just west of the village, near the Mohawk River. They, along with Earl Healy were cutting hay and Healy was driving a Reo Speedwagon truck, pulling the hay rake and other implements used for haying, to the field to be cut. The younger Reese was a passenger in the cab of the truck when suddenly, flames erupted under the cab. Both men jumped from the vehicle and ran to safety about forty feet away before turning to look back at the burning truck. Suddenly and without warning, one end of the gasoline tank blew out and struck David Reese Jr. with enough force to knock him to the ground. His clothing was saturated with gasoline and burst into flames. While in shock and pain, he unsuccessfully tried to put out the flames by rolling on the ground. He then ran nearly two hundred yards to the Mohawk River where he jumped into the water. He was able to walk to the Bargy home where an ambulance was summoned, but the severity of his burns was obvious, and he died in the Ilion hospital at 4 a.m. the next morning.

The family was devastated and the operation of the farm was now totally in the hands of now sixty-four-year-old David Reese Sr. The farm was soon put up for sale, advertisements emphasizing the fact that the property was only one half mile from the milk plant in the village. Help was needed to milk the herd and maintain the property. A thirty-two-year-old Ilion man, Leroy York, had worked previously as a farm hand and was hired by Mr. Reese. Leroy was said to be "a peculiar sort of chap" with an impediment in his speech and after being raised by the Sweet family in Ilion, he then went by the name

Leroy Sweet for that reason. Leroy proved to be a good worker when he was fully instructed in any job he was assigned. In October 1926, the cows were pastured on the easterly end of the Reese farm, far from the Reese barn and house. Leroy, who had now been working on the farm for one month, was mending the property line fences. A parcel of land adjoining the Reese farm had been purchased by Michael Camerano, a man who had migrated from Italy but had become a naturalized U.S. citizen. Mike was growing apples on his property and they became a tempting treat for the Reese cows, so much so that they broke through the fencing and consumed a considerable amount of fruit. Mike was irate and went to the Reese home to complain to David Reese Sr. David told Mike that he had assigned Leroy to repairing the fences and he instructed Mike to go directly to Leroy and show him where the fence had been broken.

But directing Mike to see Leroy proved to be a bad idea as Mike, speaking broken English and Leroy with a speech impediment met. The conversation was a recipe for disaster as both raised the tempo of the exchange to a point where it became an argument. Each man was using "unpleasant terms" towards each other. Mr. Reese arrived upon the scene and heard Leroy shout "If you want a fight, you can have it." He immediately told Leroy to keep still and the three men parted ways. But Mike felt very threatened by Leroy's actions and later visited Justice William H. Waterbury in the village, requesting a warrant be sworn out for Sweet's arrest because Mike "had been threatened with a whipping." The judge informed Camerano that there were insufficient grounds for a warrant and suggested he see a lawyer about the matter.

On the morning of October 25, 1926, Leroy Sweet's job assignment was to spread manure on the far eastern pasture, next to the Camerano orchard. He hitched the manure spreader to a team of horses he was familiar with. They were a good pair of workhorses and were gentle by nature and Leroy drove them to the remote pasture. But later in the morning, David Reese's wife, Nancy, observed the team returning to the barn and something wasn't right. Leroy appeared to be slumped over the dashboard of the wagon and lying partially on the whipple tree directly behind the horses. She ran out of the house and called to the hired hand, asking what was the matter with him. As she drew closer, it was obvious that he was seriously wounded.

Leroy was in and out of consciousness as Nancy ran to a neighbor's home to request they call Dr. Albones. When she returned, Leroy spoke, saying that he had been shot and then said "Mrs. Reese, I'm dying, my feet are getting cold." She asked who had shot him and he replied "Mike did." Dr. Albones arrived within fifteen minutes and had the wounded man transported to the Ilion Hospital by ambulance. But there was nothing that would be done in Ilion; Leroy died before the ambulance reached the hospital.

The shooting occurred beyond the boundaries of the village, so the Herkimer County Sheriff's office was called. This was the third time in two years and only two months after the killing of Frank Oliver that the Sheriff's patrol had been called to a Frankfort farm to pursue a murderer who had fled the scene of the crime. Each of the two previous shooters was still being sought at the time of this third shooting. Of course, in the village, an anxious populace emphasized the fact that all three perpetrators were "Italian." This was during a time when honest, hard-working immigrants from Europe were trying to assimilate. After Nancy Reese's statement that Leroy told her that Mike had shot him, an immediate search for Mike Camerano was begun in the area around the farm. When a tip was received that Mike had been seen in the southern section of town, fifteen deputies combed that neighborhood without success.

Just as Frank Oliver's killer was never found a few months earlier in the western section of town, Leroy's murderer remained at large following the crime. Within a few days of the shooting, Mrs. Michael Camerano and her son Joseph Camerano, were arrested on a bench warrant as material witnesses and locked up in the Herkimer County Jail. Attorney Edward J. Reilly was successful in securing the pair's release from jail. Mike and Thomas Ruffalo posted five thousand dollars bail for each. Attorney Edward J. Reilly would later go on to become a nationally known defense attorney in the Lindbergh baby murder trial, representing Richard Bruno Hauptmann, convicted of murder in that case.

Months passed and nothing indicated that Camerano was in the area. District Attorney James Green presented the case to the grand jury and Michael Camerano was indicted for first-degree murder. In January 1927, the County Board of Supervisors approved a five hundred dollar reward for information leading to an arrest. They printed and distributed posters to authorities all over the eastern U.S. bearing a picture and the caption "wanted for murder." But Mike joined Mike Catalino and Charles Ribardo, the Frankfort murderers of 1924-1926 that had successfully evaded capture.

The winter of 1926–1927 passed with no sign of Camerano. Sheriff James C. Rasbach, intent on bringing the fugitive to justice, persuaded Herkimer County supervisors to once again engage New York City detective Michael Bernabic to track down their latest fugitive. The Italian speaking sleuth from the big city had successfully captured fugitive Salvatore Polizzi for them, five years earlier. Sheriff Rasbach provided details about Camerano's family in Frankfort and Bernabic began searching for relatives known to be somewhere on Long Island. The shrewd detective put several people in the New York City area under surveillance while he made return trips to Frankfort searching for leads. He worked undercover, amongst the Italian colony, establishing the connection between local residents and the people in Long Island.

On May 27, 1927, the detective was seen in Frankfort and he was there for a good reason. While monitoring the movements of Camerano's relatives, he concluded that the wanted man had been visiting Frankfort. Bernabic would later claim that he observed Camerano entering a residence on Fourth Avenue. According to later statements, he summoned authorities to raid the residence, but they found no trace of the wanted man.

Detective Bernabic returned to the city and was informed by his partners that they had found relatives in Long Island and Brooklyn who were probably aiding and abetting the man charged with first-degree murder; that was a felony. By June 20th Bernabic pinpointed the location of a farm on Long Island possibly harboring Camerano. It was the farm of Peter and Christina Lambiaso. Peter's brother, Paul DeMarco, and two stepsons of Camerano, Michael and Martin Gurelio were also possibly involved, as were two sons of Camerano living in Brooklyn named Frank and Tony. Frank had married a daughter of his stepbrother Martin. So there were many people around New York City possibly involved in harboring the fugitive that Herkimer County was desperate to catch. But surveillance of those possibly involved uncovered no sightings of Camerano. It was decided to put legal pressure on the group to get someone to come forward with information.

A subpoena served on Paul DeMarco demanded that he appear before the Mineola, New York district attorney and disclose all locations and people pertinent to possible movements by Camerano. In July, stepsons Michael and Martin Gurello were arrested and charged by a Herkimer County Grand Jury with being accessories after a felony. They posted five thousand dollars bail each. Peter and Christina Lambiaso and Paul DeMarco were arrested on the same charge and brought to the Herkimer County Jail by Herkimer County Sheriffs. When all parties saw the seriousness of their charges, people finally began to talk.

Camerano was indeed at Valley Stream, Long Island after the crime, driven there by a son and several friends. He found a job as a night watchman with the Gibson Corporation in April 1927, using the name "John Bietsa" as an alias. The paymaster at the Gibson plant, said Bietsa was his best watchman. Mike Camerano was at the Lambiaso's farm from March to July in 1927. This information was revealed at a trial in Herkimer during January 1928 in which the defendants, Peter and Christina Lambiaso and Paul DeMarco, were held on the charge of being accessories after a felony.

During the trial, prosecutors emphasized the seriousness of the felony charges against the Long Island defendants, attempting to extract more information to pin down the location of their fugitive relative. Paul DeMarco admitted that he had told Mike about being subpoenaed and that was the event coinciding with the fugitive's disappearance from the Long Island farm. The defendants had been indicted in July, six months before the trial and that was the last time any of those on trial would admit to seeing Mike Camerano.

Admissions were made that Mike's sons had transported him between Frankfort and Long Island, and that Paul DeMarco had taxied him between Long Island and Brooklyn several times. It was revealed that the accused murderer very easily could have been taken into custody in May 1927 by a New York City policeman, Louis Noennick. The officer had dined at the same table with the fugitive in a Brooklyn restaurant and described having a conversation with a man calling himself John Bietsa. Officer Noennick knew Bietsa was at the Lambiaso farm but stated that he had no idea that Bietsa was actually Camerano and wanted on a murder charge. It was also learned that Mike had shaved off the mustache that was so prominently displayed on his wanted poster.

The four day trial in a cold Herkimer, New York courtroom during January 1928, featured some interesting presentations by both the prosecution and defense councils. James and Fred O'Donnell represented the defendants and called the whole "Long Island affair" a frame-up on the part of New York City officials who obtained statements from the defendants in a "New York City way." They claimed that Detective Michael

Bernabic could have arrested Camerano when he observed him on Fourth Avenue in Frankfort during May 1927 but wanted to prolong collection of his daily fee from Herkimer County.

District Attorney James H. Greene presented the Reeses as witnesses to establish the fact that before he died, Leroy Sweet identified Mike Camerano as the party responsible for one of Herkimer County's most brutal murders. He described Mike as waiting in hiding with a double barrel shotgun and firing both barrels, hitting Leroy in the back. Greene presented expert witnesses who were able to state that the double barrel gun found in Camerano's home fired the shells found near the scene of the shooting. Capt. William Jones of the New York City Police Department stated that the left-hand firing pin of the double barrel shotgun was homemade, while the right-hand pin was factory made. The difference made him confident that the empty casings he examined were fired by Mike Camerano's gun.

As the Long Island residents were called to the stand it became obvious that all of those arrested would once again firmly state that they all were unaware that their relative, Michael Camerano had killed a man in upstate New York. Prosecutors finally concentrated on obtaining convictions of those directly involved in actually harboring Mike; Peter Lambiaso and his wife, Christina. After thirteen hours of deliberation, the jury decided that the Lambiasos had harbored Mike at their home in Valley Stream, fully knowing that he was not John Bietsa, but was Michael Camerano, a man wanted on murder charges. At 1:30 a.m. the jury returned to the courtroom and announced to Judge Bell that they found both Peter and his wife guilty of the charge of being accessories to a felony.

Attorney James P. O'Donnell made an appeal to the court for leniency, especially for Mrs. Lambiaso, stating that she was the mother of nine children and was expecting another in a few months. Judge Bell was moved by her condition and suspended a jail sentence; she was free to return to Long Island and care for her large family. Christina hastily left the courtroom in tears after her sentence was suspended, and before the determination of her husband's punishment was handed down by the judge. The conviction of her husband, Peter, resulted in the Judge Bell's decision to sentence him to Auburn Prison for not less than fourteen months or more than eighteen months. Peter was in tears as he was led from the courtroom, knowing that he would be locked away from his family for over a year.

So, fifteen months after the crime in Frankfort, those responsible for harboring fugitive Michael Camerano were dealt with by the law; but where was the fugitive? Detective Michael Bernabic, along with his partner, Detective Bernard Greve kept the case active. Startling information about the missing man was transmitted to them by authorities in Italy. In Padula, Italy there had been an active warrant for the arrest of Michael Camerano. In April of 1892 he shot and killed his uncle, Michael DeMalto, in Padula. As a member of the Italian Army, he was on furlough when he was caught by his uncle stealing a sizable amount of money kept in the uncle's home where he was staying. It was alleged that Camerano shot his uncle, who died shortly after.

Camerano's U.S. citizenship papers showed that he migrated from Naples on May 10, 1892. After he fled Italy the case was tried in an Italian court and a conviction was found. A sentence of twenty years awaited him if he returned before thirty years from the date of the shooting. That would be 1931, just three years away, but Detective Bernabic had a hunch that Mike would leave the U.S. for his former homeland in spite of the threat to him there.

Establishing a good relationship with Italian authorities, the Italian-speaking detective gathered enough information to confidently conclude that Mike would indeed return to Italy. Nine months after the Lambiaso trial came to a conclusion, Detective Bernabic took a steamer to Italy, combining his work on another case with Italian connections and the hunt for the Frankfort fugitive. But as months went by, back in Herkimer, Sheriff James Rasbach received little news from Europe that his fugitive would ever be brought back to face the court. As a sheriff who was appointed by the governor at the time, Franklin D. Roosevelt, it would certainly be in his best interest politically if he were able to convict the fugitive in an internationally publicized case.

Black Tuesday, October 29, 1929, the day that the stock market crashed, marking the beginning of the "Great Depression" came and went and Detective Bernabic was still in Italy, having been overseas now for over a year and offering nothing new in the Camerano case. But during 1930, Sheriff Rasbach received telegrams stating that the famous detective was on the trail of the Frankfort murderer. Bernabic assured Rasbach that Mike Camerano had returned to his hometown of Padula in southern Italy. When Mike was a boy growing up there, the village had a population of nine thousand residents but had experienced a loss of thousands due to migration. By 1930, less than five thousand lived there.

Mike had gone back to his hometown and Detective Bernabic found him. Now the process to extradite him would begin; an historic event in itself. No person who had left Italy, became a naturalized American citizen and then returned to Italy had ever been given up to be taken back to the United States to face criminal charges. Additionally, by the time Mike was found, the statute of limitations had been exceeded in the Italian court system for the charges against him in the shooting of his uncle.

Taken into custody by Detective Bernabic and Italian authorities, Mike was arrested and jailed in Salerno, but later transferred to Naples to await the arrival of authorities from the United States once Italy granted the right to extradite. Herkimer County District Attorney James H. Greene initiated the request for a warrant to Governor Roosevelt who successfully obtained the signature of President Herbert Hoover on documents later sent to the Italian government. Permission to return the prisoner was quickly granted once it was revealed that Camerano's murder charge in his hometown could no longer be prosecuted.

On October 13, 1930, four years after the murder of Leroy Sweet took place, Herkimer County Sheriff J. Collingwood Rasbach and his wife traveled to Italy on a steamship, along with Deputy Sheriff Adam M. Allen, to take custody of Michael Camerano in Naples and return the naturalized citizen to the U.S. to face trial in Herkimer County Court. Sheriff

Rasbach would then become the first American police official to successfully extradite a fugitive from Italy. They were accompanied by Detective Bernabic on the voyage home, traveling on the liner Saturnia. It was another month until the prisoner was turned over to Herkimer County officials. Once in New York Harbor, Camerano was taken off the ship in quarantine and taken to the Barge Office by cutter where District Attorney Greene and Deputy Sheriffs Farrell and Grady were waiting to take charge of the fugitive.

The now sixty-year-old alleged murderer was transported by automobile to the Herkimer County Jail where a large group of newspaper reporters had gathered. Those reporters seized upon facts revealed by Detective Bernabic to Sheriff Rasbach while the two were in Italy. Italian authorities told the shrewd detective that in addition to the murder of his uncle, Michael Camerano's personal life contained several interesting chapters. Before he had first left for America he married in Italy and left that wife behind. Once in Frankfort he married again and had two children with that wife. But the most amazing piece of information uncovered by Bernabic was that upon fleeing the United States and returning to Italy, he again married, this time to a twenty-six-year-old woman. At the time of Mike's capture his new woman was nearly nine months pregnant!

Mike sat in his jail cell for four months awaiting trial on first degree murder charges. Reporters injected irony into the story, suggesting that perhaps he was contemplating what was worse, facing a fate of dying in the electric chair or facing his Frankfort wife. He told reporters that because he had received no letters from his American wife, he thought she had rejected him. But she did visit him in his cell and even brought a woolen blanket for him to keep warm in his cold surroundings. He was kept in the same cell that previously held infamous murderer, Chester Gillette.

By January 1931, prisoner Camerano was said to have become despondent and was acting irrationally. Authorities brought in Dr. George Barnes to examine him. The doctor's conclusion pointed to the several weeks that Mike sat alone in his cell, giving Mike time to contemplate his fate. He now knew that he would face Justice Miller in April on a first degree murder charge that, if found guilty, would send him to the electric chair. The doctor stated that over time, Mike would probably be himself again.

The doctor's opinion proved correct and soon District Attorney Greene, newly elected Sheriff Leo Lawrence, and Mike's appointed attorney, Chester J. Winslow began a dialog with the defendant in preparation for the impending trial. Mike began to talk and admitted that he committed the crime during a bout of extreme anger over the failure of Leroy Sweet to cooperate with him in repairing the broken fence that was allowing cows from the Reese farm into his apple orchard. He revealed that when he left his relatives in Long Island, he moved to Boston where he earned enough money to pay for a trip to Italy. He had received word that his mother was dying in Padula. But problems seemed to follow Mike; after his mother passed he got into argument with his brother over the family property and he left Padula.

Before his trial was to take place, Mike agreed to a plea bargain proposed by the district attorney. On March 21, 1931 Michael Camerano plead guilty to murder in the second degree before Justice Edmund H. Lewis of Syracuse. The need for a long and expensive trial was no longer necessary. County officials were elated; the four year search had cost the county treasury a sizable expenditure.

Justice Lewis sentenced Mike to a term of twenty years to life at Auburn Prison. His age was then sixty-one years and he would no doubt spent the remainder of his life behind bars. At Auburn, the former Frankfort resident continued to provide news reporters with unexpected material. Prison officials revealed that when they assigned a number to Mr. Camerano, the next identifier to be used was 44,444. This was the first time in fifteen years that identical digits came up. One reporter suggested that maybe Camerano would be just naturally lucky at poker.

Back in Herkimer a controversy remained over reimbursing the officials involved in bringing Mike back to the U.S. The sheriff had brought his wife along on the trip and paid her way. But some questioned bills submitted for five days at a hotel in Paris, France, seven days at a Hotel In Rome, Italy and seven days at a hotel in Naples. Many still remembered Attorney O'Donnell's charge that Detective Bernabic could have captured his man four years earlier on Forth Avenue in Frankfort but was trying to prolong his per diem payments in the case. The cost to capture and try Michael Camerano was said to be unprecedented in county history.

Payment to Detective Michael Bernabic had been delayed for years, resulting in the New York City detective finally initiating a Supreme Court civil action against Herkimer County in Bronx County, New York. It was over five years after he had been hired to capture the fugitive that Bernabic would finally be paid, but his bill for five thousand eight hundred dollars (almost ninety thousand dollars today) was reduced by the Herkimer County Board of Supervisors to four thousand, one hundred and fifty dollars. At the sentencing, Michael Camerano's assigned attorney, Chester Winslow of Frankfort, told Justice Lewis that the admitted murderer had simply lost his temper when confronted by an uncooperative Leroy Sweet in the pasture of the Reese farm. The Justice quickly reminded Winslow that his client had also killed his uncle in Italy years earlier and it was time that Mr. Camerano be removed from society.

Chapter 12

Coco DiMaggio's Murder 1931

During the first half of the twentieth century, the area surrounding the Frankfort Railroad Depot (which sat just north of Orchard Street and south of Sheldon Avenue) became the section of the village where new immigrants located. After arriving from New York City by train they were greeted by friends and relatives speaking their native language. Sheldon Avenue, Railroad Street and Orchard Street were soon filled with apartment houses where almost everyone spoke Italian and the second generation became fluent in both Italian and English. An intense campaign to rid the Mohawk Valley of a small group who had come to this country with the intention of carrying on the practices of the Black Hand Society was successful and by 1930 most of that activity had ceased. But the prohibition era, combined with the beginning of the Great Depression led to illegal activity associated with supplying a thirsty public with homemade alcohol. Many stores and saloons in the village were successfully raided by federal agents and many residents knew that "they were making alcohol below the tracks." At 106 Orchard Street, the store operated by Bennie Zito was a hub of activity in the immigrant community that surrounded it. Around 1925, Zito's establishment was called a "soft drink" place, but would later be called a grocery store and pool room.

On Christmas night in 1925, Officers Engert and Barnett of the Frankfort Police Department surprised a group of card players in the back of the store, confiscating only two dollars and forty-five cents as evidence of illegal gambling. The case against Bennie Zito, charging him with maintaining a room for gambling, dragged on until April. He was represented by a village attorney, Chester Winslow, but a jury found him guilty as charged. In 1927, another raid, this time by New York State Troopers, found illegal alcohol in the store. That raid led to County Judge Charles Bell signing an order to confiscate a revolver that Zito carried legally, revoking his permit to own a handgun. Permits required to purchase a handgun were easy to obtain in those days and the irony at the time was the fact that members of the Frankfort Police Department privately sold guns to the public. Wallace Newton, a former village police chief admitted in court that he had sold almost two hundred handguns to residents.

Six years after the card game raid at Zito's, a game held on the evening before Columbus Day in 1931 became the focal point of a murder investigation. The crime was brutal. An unidentified body was discovered at 1:20 a.m. lying in a pool of blood on the middle of the sidewalk at Railroad Street. Three young Frankfort men who had spent the night at a dance in Mohawk were returning to their homes at Orchard and Railroad Streets and as they walked over the five sets of railroad tracks that crossed Railroad Street at the time, the three made the atrocious discovery.

The crime scene was directly in front of William H. Van Deusen's Coal Yard. Called "boys" in the morning paper, Sam Minosh, Joseph Tripoli and James Gelose found the body lying face down and immediately notified the patrolman on duty. Officer Leo Skevnick had heard the shots but was unaware of the fatal shooting until the three young men told him about their discovery of the body. Police Chief Thomas Jackson was notified and immediately called the Herkimer County Sheriff's Department, State Police and City of Utica detectives to help with the investigation. Sheriff Leo Lawrence took command of the crime scene, joined by Lieutenant Cosart of the state police and Utica detective Fred Greico.

For a few hours, the identity of the victim was unknown and when questioned, neighbors in the immediate vicinity of the crime scene "knew nothing." Salvatore Paratore said he retired at 10:30 p.m. that evening and heard nothing during the night to disturb him. Mrs. Jennie Spina said she retired at 9:00 p.m. and told police she heard no shots that night. A quest to place an identity on the victim began with examination of what was found on his person. Just a few dollars in cash, several Italian cigar butts and a religious picture about six by ten inches, neatly folded, were all that was found. The dead man was only about five foot six inches tall and carried a black umbrella with a crooked handle. His belt buckle bore the initial "D." A label in his coat showed that it was purchased from the Martin Clothing Store in Brooklyn, New York.

Investigators discovered several clues that gave them an idea of how the victim met his fate. A trail of blood began south of the railroad tracks and led to where the body was found, north of the tracks. One mushroomed bullet was found on the sidewalk but the man had been shot several times in the head. No bullet casings were found, suggesting a revolver was the murder weapon. In the road, about a foot from the curb and directly opposite of where the body was discovered, were fresh skid marks from an automobile and a small puddle of radiator fluid, suggesting a car had stopped suddenly. At this point, investigators suspected a drive-by shooting related to illegal bootlegging activity in the immediate neighborhood which was already the subject of an undercover investigation. That conclusion led Corporal Fitzpatrick and Trooper Doyle to begin a widespread search for an automobile but that proved unproductive.

By around 3:30 a.m., a neighbor came forward and told police on the scene that he knew who the victim was. Peter Caiola of 218 Railroad Street claimed the dead man was Calogero DiMaggio, a forty-one year old man who had migrated from Italy and was known as Coco. Nine years previous he had married Clara Tocco and now went by the name Nicholas DiMaggio. He supported his family of six by operating a truck farm in East Schuyler.

At 4:30 a.m., both Sheriff Leo Lawrence and Frankfort Police Chief Thomas Jackson went to the DiMaggio home, only a block away, at 129 Sheldon Avenue. They encountered Clara DiMaggio who was up and awaiting the return of her husband. Upon hearing the news of her husband's fate she became hysterical but was able to give the officers information about the time period when Coco had left the house. She claimed her husband had left the house around 6:30 p.m. to take a walk. Before he left she warned him about going out in the cold night air because he was suffering from a bad cold. He told her that he would take a walk and return and she became very worried when he never returned home. As word of the shooting spread throughout the neighborhood, dozens of friends and relatives came to console the woman now a widow, left to raise four small children; Julio 7, Joseph 6, Lena 2, and Florence 1.

Now that the victim had an identity, police detectives began interrogating relatives. Clara's two brothers, James and Sam Tocco were taken to Herkimer for questioning by District Attorney Carl W. Peterson, Lieutenant Cosart and Sheriff Leo Lawrence. They sought Information to build a foundation with the facts required to solve the case, asking about where Coco socialized in the village and who he associated with. An inquest was begun by Coroner James W. Graves at the Owens Funeral Home. The autopsy revealed that before Coco was shot he was hit on the head with a blunt instrument and after he fell face downward on the sidewalk, five shots from a .32 caliber revolver were emptied into his head at close range from the right side of his head. A large bruise was found on his left shoulder. This was truly a horrific crime for the small village.

The most significant question to be answered in the minds of investigators was "where was Coco DiMaggio coming from when he walked along Railroad Street toward his home after midnight?" Bennie Zito's store was the obvious place to start; it was only a few hundred feet from the murder scene. But the silence in the Italian colony was predictable. People were terrified and rightly so, the fear of retribution was instilled in the minds of those who had lived through the Black Hand era. Detective Fred Greico of the Utica Police Department was able to calm some fears by speaking to the immigrants in Italian and soon found out that indeed, Coco had been in a card game in Bennie Zito's store and had probably left when the game broke up.

With that information in hand, State and Herkimer County law officers moved with every means available at the time to "haul in" and interrogate anyone who had been at Zito's that evening. There was no reading of Miranda Rights in those days and officers could place anyone in a lockup while questioning them. The investigation went on for several weeks and it was surmised that quite a bit of information was acquired that would tie the killing to bootlegging activity in the vicinity of the crime scene. Within a month, a grand jury's report released on November 25th showed no indictments in the DiMaggio case but a large scale roundup by authorities was thought to have gathered in many of the key players.

The sheriff, along with the district attorney and coroner, were successful in having County Judge Abram Zoller issue an order to hold six Frankfort residents in the county jail as material witnesses. At the same time, they (along with federal agents) carried out raids on three large stills, all within a block of the DiMaggio home. In the rear of Mike Cokiara's home at 312 Railroad Street, a 750 gallon alcohol cleaning plant was found in full operation. "Cleaning" meant attempting to get a multitude of poisons out of the moonshine being produced. During 1926, five hundred people died in New York City of alcohol poisoning. The operator, John Caruso of Utica, was alone in the barn with hundreds of gallons of alcohol. He was arrested and taken to the county jail. The next raid took place in the rear of Mike Sciortino's William Street home. Again, hundreds of unattended gallons of alcohol were found. The third raid took place back on Railroad Street, very close to the crime scene, under Charles Damico's home where a beer plant was found containing 1800 gallons of beer mash and several barrels of finished product. Although the raids took place near the DiMaggio home, nothing could be found to connect the illegal activity to the murdered man. The processing equipment discovered was owned by bootleggers from the City of Utica who were probably renting buildings in Frankfort to avoid detection by city police and federal dry agents headquartered in Utica.

The Frankfort residents held in the Herkimer County Jail as material witnesses were assigned extraordinary bail amounts by Judge Zoller. Every individual determined to be a card player in the game that included the murdered man in Bennie Zito's establishment on the night of the shooting, was arrested and locked up, including Bennie Zito. The amount of bail for Antonio (Anthony) DiPiazza and Constantino (Stephen) Prestigiacomo, the two men who finally admitted leaving the premises with Coco DiMaggio, were each assigned a bail of $100,000.

Thomas DeJohn, Philip Corona and Gaetano Antonucci had only participated in the card game with DiMaggio and were assigned $5000 bail each, but Bennie Zito was ordered held in $50,000 bail. These bail amounts were explained by Judge Zoller as due in part by the lack of cooperation of residents in the neighborhood with the police. It had taken a month to establish who the card players were that night. The lofty extent of the bail judgments made it impossible for all but the three assigned a $5000 bail to be able to leave the county jail. That amount in 1931 would be equal to $77,000 in these times. A $50,000 bail then would be equivalent to $770,000 today and the $100,000 amount would equal $1.5 million dollars today. Those lofty figures led James P. O'Donnell and Chester J. Winslow, attorneys representing the jailed witnesses, to seek a drastic reduction in the bail requirements. DiPiazza, Prestigiacomo and Zito had been locked up two weeks when a show cause order was made to Judge Zoller.

District Attorney Peterson's testimony at the bail hearing persuaded Judge Zoller to deny the motion to reduce bail after the defense attorneys had unsuccessfully presented the two held in $100,000 bond as working men, making $25 per week and having large families, one with five children and one with six children. In denying the motion, Judge Zoller stated that the confinement of the witnesses in jail would keep them free from harm. District Attorney Peterson concluded by stating that "they don't want to be implicated in the thing for their lives might be in danger and bail has been fixed according to the value of their testimony."

The county's round-up of witnesses led to some unusual actions on the part of the district attorney. Store owner Bennie Zito's incarceration in the Herkimer County Jail included confinement of his wife and nine-year-old son Jack. They had been in Herkimer two weeks when Mrs. Zito's father, Peter Sarmi, hired lawyer Charles B. Hane to petition the court with a writ of habeas corpus to determine if authorities had the right to detain the Zitos. When the hearing was held, Sheriff Leo Lawrence informed the court that Mrs. Zito and her son had already been released and he claimed that Bennie Zito was confined in jail purely on his own accord. He also claimed that the trio came to Herkimer voluntarily in order to be questioned regarding the DiMaggio murder and that their stay in the county jail was voluntary. After that testimony was given, the proceedings were dismissed.

In the first week of December, Attorneys O'Donnell and Winslow applied for a writ of certiorari in another attempt to reduce bail for DiPiazza and Prestigiacomo. A writ of certiorari orders a lower court to deliver its record in a case to a higher court for review. In this case, that would be a special session of Supreme Court in Herkimer to be held by Justice Edward N. Smith. At that session, Judge Smith first indicated that he thought the bail set was excessive but wanted to hear the arguments by both the defense and prosecution. O'Donnell claimed that Prestigiacomo was not present when DiMaggio was killed and should not have even been held as a witness. But District Attorney Peterson argued that they should both be held because "every day we read about witnesses being bumped off." He cited similar cases where witnesses to a crime had been "eliminated" by groups. Because he was held in jail, Judge Edmund Lewis denied Prestigiacomo citizenship at a naturalization proceeding held in Herkimer on December 6th, on the grounds that his record showed "he was not well disposed".

Supreme Court Judge Smith had strong words regarding the silence of people. "The attitude of silence is something more than silence of fear. It is silence of habit, something that has been put in the minds through years of discipline. That is contrary to the laws of America and is forcing us into actions which ordinarily would not be approved. The people should inform the law of what they know."

The arguments made by the defense attorneys failed to persuade Judge Smith to reduce the bail amounts and the three witnesses held on the highest bail remained confined well into the month of December. In spite of the sheriff's earlier statement that Zito's confinement was voluntary, he was held on the $50,000 amount. On December 20, 1931, Zito's nearly two month incarceration was ended when Attorney James Bennison presented a bond for the full amount of bail, furnished by thirty-five property owners from Frankfort. Mrs. Zito had promised their five children a Christmas Tree if "daddy got out."

As the pair still being held spent the holidays behind bars, their attorneys announced a plan to take the complaint of excessive bail to the Appellate Court at Rochester. The appeal was sought from the decisions of both Judge Zoller and Judge Smith. The Appellate Division session would begin in January 1932 and on January 22nd. a decision by that court was received by county authorities directing them to release both men. The court had found that holding the two witnesses on an excessive bail amount was contrary to laws at the time. But just prior to receiving the order to release the prisoners, Sheriff Lawrence shocked the press by announcing that Anthony DiPiazza had furnished a confession stating that it was he who had murdered Coco DiMaggio. His brother-in-law, Steven Prestigiacomo was immediately released and DiPiazza was arraigned on a murder charge.

The Italian community was more confused than shocked after hearing that DiPiazza had confessed, just as he was ready to be released from jail, but this would be sorted out when he was brought to trial. Confessing meant DiPiazza, who had already spent three months in jail would remain in a cell another three months until his trial would begin. During the trial that finally took place in May 1932, the details of how a confession was obtained would be revealed.

Six months after Coco DiMaggio's body was found lying on the Railroad Street sidewalk, a jury was summoned for the first degree murder trial of Anthony DiPiazza. The event would be full of surprises. Herkimer County authorities boasted that this was the first murder involving Italians to be solved in the county since 1919. But then it was revealed that the actual confession that solved the case was obtained by Amsterdam, New York resident, Police Lieutenant Joseph Genova, a hired detective that normally worked for the New York Central Railroad Police and had a reputation for his ability to solve homicide cases. On December 2nd 1931 District Attorney Carl W. Peterson wrote a letter to the chief of the New York Central police asking that Genova be granted a leave of sixty days to work for Herkimer County. Permission was granted and Genova interrogated both DiPiazza and Prestigiacomo during their Herkimer confinement. Felix Di Martini, a former New York City detective, had also been hired by D.A. Peterson earlier and had interrogated the duo before they were incarcerated in Herkimer.

DiPiazza's confession showed that Prestigiacomo, DiPiazza and the victim DiMaggio left Bennie Zito's together, but at the corner of Railroad and Orchard Sts., Prestigiacomo continued east on Orchard St. to his home, while DiPiazza and DiMaggio traveled north along Railroad St. At the railroad crossing,

DiPiazza claimed he got into a heated quarrel with DiMaggio, pulled out his revolver and fired five bullets into his friend's head.

At the initial examination of DiPiazza that began on March 1st, the defendant's attorney was unsuccessful in persuading Justice of the Peace Clarence Van Horn to release the alleged statements made by DiPiazza to police. Mrs. DiPiazza and the couple's six children were in attendance at that hearing. Jury selection for the first degree murder trial began on April 25, 1932 before Supreme Court Justice Edmund H. Lewis of Syracuse. Utica attorney William Rose Lee, joined James P. O'Donnell in defending Anthony DiPiazza. Once again, the defendant's wife and six children were present in a courtroom filled to capacity, many spectators arriving very early in the morning.

The prosecution presented New York City Detective Felix DiMartini who produced a statement signed by DiPiazza less than a month after the murder, but before DiPiazza was in custody in the Herkimer County Jail. In that statement, DiPiazza denied he was in Bennie Zito's place on October 11th and claimed that he had spent the day with his family. It was a typewritten statement and was signed by DiPiazza, Sheriff Leo Lawrence, Lieutenant Cosart of the state police and detective DiMartini. Because the card players at Zito's that night had given statements admitting they had played cards and that DiPiazza was in the game, the prosecution established the fact that DiPiazza lied in his statement, contradicting the testimony of six other people.

Bennie Zito took the stand and testified that DiPiazza came into his store the day after the card game and said

"Too bad what happened last night." He followed that with "When I left your store last night, I saw two men in an automobile shoot DiMaggio, and then drive away." Zito told the court, "DiPiazza and DiMaggio were always good friends, just like brothers." Following Zito's testimony, every man who admitted to being in the card game testified and said that DiPiazza had played in that game.

Jail Turnkey Charles Daniels made a strong point for the prosecution when he testified that he heard DiPiazza declare twice that he had killed his friend. He claimed the defendant said "I killed Coco and I'm glad it's over." Daniels heard those words from DiPiazza's mouth on the same day in January that DiPiazza signed the statement now presented as DiPiazza's confession. Daniels said DiPiazza made a second verbal confession later by saying "I'm glad its over; I killed Coco. I put five bullets in him; if I had two hundred, I would have put them in him."

But Attorney O'Donnell told the jury that DiPiazza's confession was coerced by strong armed tactics by the state police and detectives that involved emotional and physical abuse. He claimed the defendant had been deprived of food and sleep for several days and not allowed to see any members of his family. When O'Donnell questioned Genova about his methods used to obtain a confession, he accused the railroad detective of making disparaging statements during the interrogation. "Did you tell the defendant that DiMaggio was no good, had improper relations with DiPiazza's wife and had killed a man in Madison, Wisconsin?" Genova gave an emphatic "no" to all of O'Donnell's questions and he denied he told DiPiazza he could get out on a self-defense plea. Physical abuse of the defendant made during the interrogations leading to the confession was denied by all of those involved in the questioning, but DiPiazza claimed he was beaten and showed bruises on his body and a missing tooth he said was a result of physical punishment inflicted on him before he signed a confession that he now said he did not recognize.

The defense team presented several prisoners who had been incarcerated during the period of the alleged abuse of the defendant. Each man testified that they had seen the defendant placed in the women's section of the jail and had observed Police Lieutenant Genova and state troopers going in and out of that section for two days. All testified that they had heard crying and hollering that kept them from sleeping properly on those nights. Stephen Prestigiacomo was placed on the stand by the defense but was not allowed to testify to being beaten in the county jail.

The prosecution then presented firearms expert J. Henry Fitzgerald of Hartford, Connecticut who gave testimony that each of the bullets taken from the victim's body or nearby were fired from the same gun, a Smith & Wesson .32 caliber revolver. The district attorney tied in that revelation with testimony given by former Frankfort Police Chief Wallace Newton that he had sold Anthony DiPiazza a Smith & Wesson revolver six years prior. But in a surprise move, the defense team presented Albert Hamilton, a ballistics expert from Auburn, New York. His testimony was in direct contradiction to that of Mr. Fitzgerald. He produced a strong microscope and showed a very interested jury that markings on the bullets showed that two were all-lead Remington bullets and were fired from an Iver-Johnson revolver, while the remaining bullets may have been fired from a Rand & Richardson revolver. His testimony was immediately discredited by the prosecution who claimed he was no more than the owner of a drugstore in Auburn. But Mr. Hamilton claimed he had testified in hundreds of cases as a ballistics expert, both on the defense and prosecution sides.

Some excitement was caused when DiPiazza, while being questioned by District Attorney Carl Peterson about his charge that he was beaten to obtain a confession, pointed a finger at State Police Corporal Doran and yelled out "there he is, he's the man who beat me." This was followed immediately by a statement made by DiPiazza's brother-in-law, Stephen Prestigiacomo, to a man setting next to him that could by heard by some in the courtroom. He stated that he too was hit by the trooper while confined in jail as a material witness. Judge Lewis said that he had not heard the remark and admonished Prestigiacomo that he make no further demonstrations in court.

Two weeks into the trial it seemed like both sides had presented evidence sufficient to decide DiPiazza's fate. But as a conclusion neared, a surprise witness took the stand for the defense. A young man named Patsy Petrell testified that he had witnessed the shooting on Railroad Street. He was allowed to describe what he supposedly had seen the night of the murder. He claimed he had no watch and was unable to tell the jury the time in the early morning that he observed the murder, only that it was after midnight.

Everyone in the courtroom listened to his story intensely as it was a complete surprise to all but the two defense attorneys. "I was walking home from a relative's house on Bee Street and approached the corner of Sheldon Avenue and Railroad Street. As I turned south on Railroad Street I observed an automobile near Van Dusen's coal shed. I heard several shots and saw two men get into a car and one man run toward me. I feared for my life and immediately ran back on Sheldon Avenue to Frankfort Street where I crossed the railroad tracks and continued to Main Street and home." He stated that he did not know any of the men he observed.

This witness had never come forward to tell his story for over six months of the murder investigation and the prosecution jumped at the chance to question him. The cross examination was conducted by District Attorney Carl Peterson. "Did you see men get out of the car?" "No, I saw men get into the car." "Did you watch what happened after you heard shots?" "Yes." "You say you saw two men get into the auto?" "Yes." "Did you see the car start up?" "No, I started running." "Did you see anybody run down the street?" "Yes."

When questioned about his failure to report what he saw, the witness said he first told his story two weeks prior in the barber shop of James Maneen, a brother-in-law of the defendant, telling Maneen that if needed he would testify. Petrell admitted that he was present at the initial preliminary examination of DiPiazza conducted before Justice of the Peace Clarence Van Horne. "Did you talk with Judge Van Horn?" "I don't remember." "Did you tell the judge, See if you can do something for him, let him go, for he's my uncle and he has six children?" "I don't know." "Did it occur to you that with that information you might tell somebody what you knew?" "No, I didn't want to be mixed up with it."

Justice Van Horn was called by the people. He stated that he had known Petrell for three or four years and said he did remember talking with Petrell at DiPiazza's original hearing but had issued the warrant for DiPiazza's arrest. Petrell also admitted that he had served six days in the Onondaga County Penitentiary and paid a fine for income tax evasion. During the final summation by the prosecution the jury was asked to totally disregard the testimony of Patsy Petrell, presenting his testimony as incredulous.

By May 6, 1932, in the second week of trial, summations began by the defense team and prosecution. Defense Attorney William Rose Lee of Utica began a masterful presentation and the jury followed his arguments with close attention. Using the premise that the confessions were coerced, he charged that the three statements obtained from DiPiazza were secured by the use of undo force and duress. He claimed that the defendant was not allowed to rest, nor given food for five days and nights; that he was kicked and slapped by Police Lieutenant Joseph Genova and State Trooper Clarence Doran. Lee stated "We are going back to the Dark Ages when a man can be detained in jail for sixty-seven days of questioning and threatening." Lee declared that no guilty man would act as DiPiazza did when the district attorney sent for him. He described how DiPiazza came to the Court House at once when told the district attorney wanted to see him and waited several hours to meet with the D.A. He claimed DiPiazza was told he would be allowed to see his wife and six children often if "he took the blame for DiMaggio's murder."

District Attorney Carl Peterson began his summation of the case for the people by labeling many of DiPiazza's statements as totally false, beginning with his denial that he was in the card game at Zito's place. The defendant's explanation of the crime was absolutely impossible, Peterson proclaimed, due to the results of the examination that revealed placement of the bullets in DiMaggio's body. The summation consumed only two hours and it basically discredited all of DiPiazza's testimony throughout the trial. Once again, the court room was packed when the case was turned over to the jury shortly before noon.

Around 6 p.m. the jury returned to the court room and asked for instructions from Justice Edmund H. Lewis. They desired information and definitions of various verdicts which might be returned, namely first and second degree murder and manslaughter, first and second degree. They returned to their deliberations after receiving this information. At 1:53 a.m., after fourteen hours of deliberation, Anthony DiPiazza was found guilty of murder, second degree. Upon revealing the decision, foreman Fordyce Bowman of Ilion, told Justice Lewis that the jury recommended leniency. Within one hour, Lewis sentenced DiPiazza to not less than twenty years nor more than the period of his natural life at hard labor in Auburn Prison. He actually served thirteen years until he was paroled in 1945 and moved to St. Louis, Missouri. He was set entirely free in 1961 and died on November 15, 1964 less than two months after his grandson murdered a seventeen-year-old girl back in Frankfort.

For years a rumor has persisted in Frankfort that Anthony DiPiazza had "taken the fall" for the murder. Nothing seems to have come out at the trial about the skid marks and radiator fluid on the street at the scene of the crime or testimony that a vehicle was seen speeding away. Also, the victim's head trauma occurring before the shooting lacked explanation. The rumor may have credibility.

Chapter 13

Tragedy on Joslin Hill 1962

.

$\mathbb{F}$rankfort did not have a homicide for three decades following the Coco DiMaggio murder on Columbus Day in 1931. The crime that ended that quiet period took place just south of the village on Joslin Hill, an area named for the Joslin family. The hill was home to many small farmers after early settlers discovered the rich soil made the area ideal for dairy farming operations and that lead to the establishment of milk plants in the village, just a few miles away. Thirty-six Joslin family members are buried in Oak View Cemetery with gravestones that span two centuries. In the village, Aaron Joslin built the original three-story building that burned in 1912. At the time it was called Frankfort's biggest fire. Many other families joined the close knit community on the hill. One of those was a family headed by Clifton H. Ladd. He was born in Virginia and had nine brothers and sisters but he moved to the Mohawk Valley in 1933. In 1936 he married May Williams who had migrated from England with her family at the age of thirteen. The marriage produced three daughters.

Mr. Ladd's interest was in dairy farming and when an opportunity was presented to him to purchase an operating dairy on Joslin Hill, he was successful in procuring it. Sadly, it was the misfortune of the farm's owner that led him to selling the operation. Marcus Clement's wife Elizabeth died in 1937, leaving him with three small children. The Ladd family took in the children and in 1941, Mr. Clements agreed to sell his farm to the Ladds as he moved to the village and took a job with the George Corrado Milling Company. Only two years later, tragedy struck the family again when Mr. Clements was killed in a terrible automobile accident on Route 20 near Richfield Springs. The three orphans were raised by the Ladd family. Two boys eventually became farmers but left the area. Doris Clements became a foster child and continued to live with the Ladds into adulthood.

Twenty years after purchasing the farm, Clifton Ladd was doing well but could use some help as he was now in his sixties. He was approached by a young man from Utica, Richard Tuscher, who claimed that a friend of his would make a good farmhand. He said that his friend had experience in farming, having worked on farms in the Rochester area. It was later learned that Tuscher had befriended that young man named Ronald Samanka while Tuscher was working as an attendant at the Newark State School for Mental Defectives. After Samanka's release from that institution, Tuscher was able to secure farm work for Samanka in the Rochester area.

Richard Tuscher eventually left Rochester and came back to his native Utica and obtained a job working for the United States Social Security Administration. He became very active in the local church community and was well known for his work with young adult groups, providing guidance to those with problems. The well spoken young man was able to convince Mr. Ladd to hire his friend Ronald Samanka for the farmhand job on the Ladd farm, a move that Mr. Tuscher would later regret for the rest of his life.

When hired, Ronald Samanka was a strong, good looking twenty-one-year-old man who would have no problem helping Clifton Ladd in the day to day operation of the dairy farm. But after only a few weeks of farm work, Ronald's personality and actions led Mr. Ladd to have second thoughts about the person he had hired. Ladd became suspicious about his new man's past. He learned that Samanka had no family and had been institutionalized since he was six years old, released from the Newark mental hospital only a year earlier. His understanding of many things that an elementary school pupil should know was limited and his personality seemed odd.

Mr. Ladd realized that Ronald was not the farmhand he envisioned. He told the new man that he could no longer keep him working and suggested that there were many farms in the area needing help. That was proven correct and soon young Samanka was working on the Ray Combs farm near Cranes Corners, about two and a half miles from the Ladd place. But in April 1962, Mr. Combs found it necessary to fire Samanka after several neighbors complained of threats made by the young man. When he was fired, Samanka became violent and threatened Mr. Combs, but left the property without incident, returning to Utica and his friend Richard Tuscher. Once again, trying to guide Samanka in the right direction, Richard convinced him to return to the Rochester area and seek work on farms there.

The Joslin Hill neighborhood was relieved that Ronald was no longer in the area and soon forgot about him. But that relief only lasted for two months after his departure from the Combs farm. On June 24, 1962, Clifton Ladd left the barn and returned to his house after the six a.m. milking. As he left the barn he could hear screams emanating from the house. He heard the screams of both his invalid sister-in-law, Mary Wygand, and his wife May. He rushed to the second floor bedroom where he knew his wife had been sleeping. He found May on the floor at the foot of the bed, lying in a pool of blood.

Clifton's wife had been stabbed several times and was rushed by ambulance to the Ilion Hospital where she struggled for her life. Dr. George Frank determined that she had been stabbed in the back, abdomen, breasts and head, causing much internal damage. She was in very critical condition and after three days of agony she died.

Within hours of the terrible crime, State Police detectives put out a thirteen state alarm for the apprehension of Ronald Samanka for questioning about the stabbing of May Ladd and a similar stabbing that had taken place in the Town of Frankfort at Dyke Road, twelve miles from the Ladd farm, just two days previous to the Joslin Hill stabbing. Philip Surace, a thirty-two-year-old Utican was the victim of that crime. He had been stabbed eight times in both his back and chest and was deceased when found near a stretch of Dyke Road that was notorious as a convenient dumping ground for the crime world. Records show that from the 1930s to the 1980s five bodies were discovered in that same general area where the Mohawk River flows under Dyke Road.

Police quickly uncovered the connection that Samanka had with Richard Tuscher and telephoned him at his Utica home on the day of Mrs. Ladd's stabbing. A trooper asked Tuscher if he knew of the whereabouts of Ronald Samanka. His quick reply was that he had not seen Ronald for several weeks. But on Wednesday, the day that Mrs. Ladd died, troopers arrested Richard Tuscher, claiming that at the time of the phone call, Samanka was with Tuscher, inside his home. It was charged that on the day of the stabbing, Tuscher had driven Ronald from Frankfort to Utica and given him money to take a train to Rochester.

Ronald Samanka was quickly arrested at his job on a farm near Rochester and brought back to the Herkimer County Jail. His friend Richard Tuscher was ordered held in the same jail by Frankfort Justice of the Peace George Murtaugh in lieu of five thousand dollars bail. He was charged with being an accessory to a felony. Later, in September, a grand jury indicted him on that charge and after Mrs. Ladd died of her wounds, his friend Ronald Samanka would now be charged and indicted for homicide.

Shortly after questioning was begun by troopers, Ronald Samanka admitted that he stabbed Mrs. Ladd with the sharp end of a sickle blade but claimed he had no part in the fatal stabbing of Philip Surace that took place only a few days before the Joslin Hills stabbing. Hoping to tie that stabbing (definitely committed with a long bladed knife) to Samanka, police tried to discredit Samanka's claim that he stabbed Mrs. Ladd with part of an old sickle blade he found on the farm property. An immediate attempt was begun to locate a knife or an old sickle on the Ladd farm.

State Police engaged a neighbor of the Ladds, Thomas Entwistle, to mow a weedy, overgrown ten acre meadow in an attempt to locate any type of weapon. They could be seen using pitchforks in an attempt to locate something. But nothing was found.

In questioning Samanka about his motive for the crime, an amazing statement was taken. He claimed that he had returned to the farm almost a year after he had been fired by Clifton Ladd and stabbed May Ladd because he was angry at her and her foster daughter, Doris Clements, because "they had laughed at him." That statement explains the fact that only Mrs. Ladd was attacked. Doris was not at the farmhouse that day and Mrs. Ladd's vulnerable invalid sister, Mary Wygand, who was in a wheelchair was untouched, apparently because in Ronald's mind, she had never laughed at him.

When questioned, Mary Wygand told troopers that the man she saw running through the house shortly after she heard her sister's screams coming from the upstairs bedroom, was Ronald Samanka. His confession and Mary's statement would be presented to the grand jury, but he would not budge from his position that he had no involvement in the Dyke Road case. Troopers pushed to tie the two crimes together. The two stabbings had taken place within twelve miles of each other. When two young men came forward and identified Samanka as a man they had picked up as hitchhiker in the vicinity of Dyke Road on the night of the Surace stabbing, Ronald continued to maintain his innocence in that crime and was given a lie detector test, the results of which were never published.

Over a month had passed after Samanka had confessed to the Joslin Hill crime when a trooper found a hunting knife on a dirt road about a half-mile from the Ladd farmhouse. Mrs. Ray Combs identified it and claimed it was her twenty-one-year-old son's hunting knife, reported missing after Samanka had been fired from his job on their farm. Troopers said they felt strongly that Samanka had taken the knife from the Combs farm and that they never believed that Mrs. Ladd was stabbed with a sickle.

In the end, Lieut. Harry Blaisdell of the New York State Police Bureau of Criminal Investigation said, "both homicides may be connected, but we haven't been able to prove it." The Philip Surace murder remains unsolved. Indictments of both Ronald Samanka and his friend Richard Tuscher were handed up by the September grand jury and sent to the Herkimer County Court where Judge Edmund A. McCarthy would hear each case.

In August, Samanka was examined at Marcy State Hospital. Psychiatrists there found him capable of standing trial. But in November, his appointed defense counsel, Philip D. O'Donnell requested an examination by two additional psychiatrists. The request was granted by Judge McCarthy and a hearing was scheduled in November to controvert the findings of the Marcy psychiatrists. Ronald Samanka was again found capable of standing trial and he was pleading innocent to the charge of first-degree murder. He spent the winter awaiting trial and in March 1963, the prosecution allowed him to plead guilty to two counts of second-degree murder. He was sentenced to serve from 30 years to life in state prison at Attica.

Two years after he was committed to Attica, he sent a handwritten application for a writ of error to Judge McCarthy. The document claimed that he was not provided an attorney, between the time of his arrest in June 1962 and his indictment. The plea was considered but no evidence was presented that would change the outcome of the sentence imposed.

Richard Tuscher, the person responsible for bringing Samanka to the Ladd farm and who was arrested following the death of Mrs. Ladd on a charge of shielding the murderer, was released from the Herkimer County Jail after posting five thousand dollars bail. His case would not be decided for almost a year. The charge was presented to two grand juries. After the September 1962 grand jury indicted him, Judge McCarthy dismissed the charge on the grounds that it was insufficient. But the judge then directed that the case be resubmitted to another grand jury. Tuscher maintained that he was not guilty of any wrongdoing. He was supported by many friends including the pastors of several Utica churches who praised Tuscher's work with young adult groups. On March 14, 1963, in its report to Supreme Court Justice Richard Aronson of Syracuse, the grand jury said that it did not find an indictment against Mr. Tuscher.

The Joslin Hill neighborhood carried on but the tragedy affected many for a long time. Clifford Ladd retired from farming a year after losing his wife but became a beekeeper and served as an assessor for the Town of Frankfort. He passed away in the farmhouse at the age of eighty in 1983. Ronald Samanka, after spending his youth confined to state institutions, served out his sentence in state prison at Attica.

Chapter 14

The Murder of Lucie Dade 1964

Frankfort was recovering from the loss of the West Shore Railroad repair shops as the twentieth century arrived and a family named Dade from Alsace Lorraine decided to make their home in the village. New industries were filling the repair shop buildings. The Continental Tool Co., Pratt Industries and Acme Road Machinery were hiring. Albert Dade was born after the Alsace Lorraine Territory was created by the German Empire in 1871, annexed from France following a German victory in the Franco-Prusssian War. People living in the territory had the right to emigrate to France or become German nationals. Albert Dade's family, along with one hundred and twenty thousand others, moved to France. Albert married Agathe Sauner in France and the couple adopted a French girl named Lucie. In 1903, when Lucie was eight years old, the trio, along with other relatives of Albert, boarded a steamer to America. Albert was a skilled machinist and his prospect for finding a job in Frankfort was good. The future looked bright for the young family.

Albert found work in the shops and proved to be a talented and industrious person. In nine years he was able to purchase a small commercial building with a second-floor apartment on South Litchfield Street. He open a small retail operation, a confectionery store, just as his brother John had done at Frankfort Street. While Albert worked in a variety of jobs in local industries, Agathe ran the store. The couple saved their money and were able to purchase a farm south of the village. They later sold the property but continued to run the store and live in their upstairs apartment.

Nine years went by after the store was opened and Albert was still working a variety of jobs while his wife ran the store. He took a job with the West Shore Railroad; it still had quite a presence in town. His first position was working with the "ice house gang", a crew that packed ice in railway cars that carried meat. That job led to his becoming the yard night watchmen. He patrolled the perimeter of railroad property in the village. The railroad still had a roundhouse repair shop, foundry and railroad station. As described in detail in Chapter 8, Albert was murdered in the railroad yard, shot with a thirty-eight caliber pistol and his killer was never brought to justice.

Agathe and Lucie were left to operate the store, but Lucie was now 26 years old and married to Renee Bolle. Agathe ran the store for many years to support herself, but life was never the same without Albert. Twenty-two lonely years went by and on April 18, 1943, Lucie came home from church services in Sts. Peter's and Paul's Church at Second Avenue and discovered the woman who had adopted her in France, now sixty-nine years old, lying motionless in the bathtub. Dr. H.J. Sheffield was called and he confirmed that she had died.

Coroner C.C. Whittemore was called in and ruled that Agathe had drowned, most likely by suicide. Another tragedy in the small Dade family. Lucie married again, this time to William Rockwell but soon lost her second husband and married again to Jack Forrester, who had come to Frankfort the year that Agathe died. He passed away in 1959 at the age of fifty-nine, so Lucie was again alone.

She continued to operate the store that had now been Dade's Variety for forty-seven years. In 1964 the store had been open for over fifty years and Lucie continued serving Frankfort's younger population with a place to buy candy and toys. Jack was gone and no longer fixing bikes when chains came off or a tire went flat, but the variety of candy and cap pistols was still there and Lucy still enjoyed coming downstairs when someone rang the bell under the sign that said "Ring front doorbell once only, be down at once." She would open the store at 8 a.m. and usually answer the bell until 8 p.m.

After the tragedy she had encountered in her life with her adopted parents and then losing three husbands, Lucie deserved a good retirement, but she chose to carry on the tradition of the store as it was now into its next fifty years. But on February 20, 1964, she would suffer the same fate that her adopted father suffered forty-three years earlier. Among Lucie's best customers were three young men in the Spine family that lived just south of the store. Nick was eleven, Mike was fifteen and Joe was a twenty-one-year-old adult. Nick had gone to the store several times in the afternoon, but the door was locked and when he rang the bell once as instructed by the sign, Lucie failed to come downstairs.

He told his oldest brother about his attempts to get Lucie to answer the bell and together, they were still unable to get a response. Patrolmen Joseph Puleo was at the intersection of Main and Litchfield Streets directing traffic. Joe Spine, who would later become Trooper Spine, notified Puleo and they went to the store together to investigate. They went around the building, peering through windows and saw that the store had been ransacked. It appeared that there was a body lying on the floor in a storeroom at the back of the store.

Police Chief George Grates was called and the building entered. The lifeless beaten body of Lucie Dade Forrester was what they had seen through the storeroom window. Chief Grates immediately called in the New York State Police. The Herkimer County Coroner, Gilbert Upright, determined that the woman was murdered between 10 p.m. and midnight on the night before the body was discovered.

Coroner Upright said that she had died of strangulation, but noted that she had been struck on the head and neck, suffering a broken larynx. Lucie's hands and feet were tied behind her back with baling twine and her mouth gagged with a silk stocking. The village was shocked that the kind and innocent senior citizen had suffered such a horrific beating before she died. Lieutenant Warren B. Surdam, the chief investigator for the State Police Bureau of Criminal Investigation released these details of the crime:

"Our investigation indicates that Mrs. Dade's fight for her life started about three feet from the front door of the store. Her glasses were found on the floor at that spot. There was a struggle along a path to the back of the store and into the small storage room behind the store area where she died."

Store items, cartons and papers were strewn along the path leading to the storeroom and the body was almost buried with debris. Lieutenant Surdam called in a half-dozen troopers to sort through the mess, both in the store and in the upstairs apartment that was found totally ransacked. A locksmith was brought in to open a small safe. It contained two bank books, some keys and personal papers. Surdam said the bank books showed "a normal amount of cash." He was convinced that two men were involved and that they probably didn't find what they were looking for. He concluded that Mrs. Dade did not keep large amounts of cash in the building.

Interviews with neighbors provided speculation on why the attack occurred. In January 1963, a fire occurred in the building next to Dades Variety. At one point, it appeared that the fire might spread to Lucie's building and she became quite anxious, telling bystanders that she should remove three hidden metal boxes from her building because they contained valuables. She was relieved when the fire was contained to the neighboring building without damaging the store and no more was said about the hidden boxes. But did someone who heard her story about the boxes think the contents were so valuable that they would later commit such a terrible crime? State police did find the three hidden boxes. They contained some jewelry, a small amount of cash and personal papers. Nothing valuable enough to kill for.

The senseless crime was never solved. The last person to see Lucie alive was Michael Spine. He had gone to the store at about 8:30 p.m. Wednesday night to get some change. When he passed by a half-hour later he noticed the lights were still on. He told police that later that night he had heard dogs barking, looked out a window in his home and saw two men running across a backyard. He claimed he thought he saw one of the men carrying a piece of pipe. Later that night, probably after the crime was committed, the store lights were off. During the investigation, state police interviewed Mrs. George Winckel who lived nearby. She said she had talked to Lucie on Wednesday afternoon. Lucie had told her that two strangers had been in the store twice on Tuesday night and just looked around, never making a purchase. She said they returned after she closed the store and rang the bell, but she did not let them in. If they were truly strangers to the area, the theory of the three hidden boxes that she mentioned during the fire a year earlier becomes less likely.

What did arouse an interest with investigators was a case in the city of Utica that occurred just seven months prior to the Frankfort murder. Mrs. Lillian Mishlanie, a widow, and the same age as Lucie Dade Forrester, was found beaten to death behind her grocery store at Sunset Avenue in the city. Her face was smashed beyond recognition and similar to Lucie, she lived in an apartment above her store. Her killer (or killers) were never determined.

Lucie Dade Forrester left no relatives, but over two hundred people attended her funeral mass in St. Mary's Church. In the end, the lives of every member of the family of three that left France seeking a new life in America, ended tragically.

Chapter 15

The Murder of Noreen Jones 1964

George Jones grew up in Scranton, Pennsylvania, one of five boys in the Jones family, a family that was split up after their father passed away at an early age. George ended up in New York City where he soon met Flora Durse. She was attending Columbia University. They married and later settled in the Mohawk Valley. Flora went on to graduate from Utica's St. Elizabeth School of Nursing and Syracuse University, attaining a masters degree in nursing. She came from a large Frankfort family that included ten children; nine were girls. "Gomer", as George was called by the many friends he made in the valley, worked at Sperry-Rand UNIVAC and in the Ilion school system. Both were industrious, hard working folks; they bought a home on West Main Street in Ilion where they would raise two boys and a girl. The girl, born in 1946, was named Noreen. When Noreen entered her freshman year in high school, the personable, quiet and athletic young lady had many friends. Her love of children was leading her on a path to enter the teaching profession. But she left the

Ilion school system and transferred to St. Mary's Academy in Little Falls for her senior year, graduating with a small class of thirty-seven students in June 1964.

Transferring to another school became necessary three years after a chance meeting that occurred at the Frankfort Municipal Swimming Pool in the summer of 1961. After finishing her freshman year in Ilion, Noreen met Benedict Xavier DiPiazza and her activities were altered negatively for the duration of her life. "Bennie", who would graduate from high school in Frankfort in 1962, was hired by the village as a lifeguard. He was the son of Mr. and Mrs. Benjamin S. DiPiazza of Pleasant Avenue in Frankfort. The senior DiPiazza was the son of Anthony DiPiazza, sent to prison in 1932 for the second-degree murder of Nicholas DiMaggio (chapter 12). He and his five siblings sat along-side their mother during the opening of his father's trial, but as an adult he rose from those circumstances to obtain an associate degree from Utica College, open an insurance business, was elected to the school board and was elected by village residents to the position of police judge.

Noreen's aunt, Frances Irons, married state trooper Allen Irons and they purchased a home just a few houses north of the municipal swimming pool. Noreen was on summer vacation and came to Frankfort to visit. Frances invited her to accompany her two young cousins on a trip to the pool. Noreen loved children and jumped at the chance to take Mary Jo, 6, and Jana, 3, to the pool.

Noreen could have never imagined that an innocent trip to the swimming pool would change her life forever. She was seen for the first time by lifeguard Bennie DiPiazza. He was soon to be finished with high school, but Noreen was only a freshman and had three more years remaining before she would graduate. Bennie was infatuated with her and prematurely expressed an interest in dating her. From that day forward it seemed to be a one-sided story, Bennie pursuing her, while she attempted to slow his advances. She avoided coming to Frankfort, but he sought her out in Ilion. From 1961 to 1964, whenever their paths crossed, the scene was always the same. Bennie wanted to make plans for marriage after Noreen graduated from high school but her interest was to pursue a career in teaching and that meant going to college upon graduation, not getting married.

In September 1962 Bennie wrecked a car in Ilion and ended up in the Ilion Hospital. Noreen visited him for about thirty minutes out of sympathy, but was still rejecting his ideas about a relationship. Wrecking the car was a serious matter and resulted in five traffic violations. His father posted one hundred dollars bail and Judge Curtis assessed him a ninety-five dollar fine and suspended his operators license for seven months. The ruling was appealed, but in April 1963, Herkimer County Judge Edmund McCarthy upheld the decision.

Bennie's persistent actions in attempting to win over Noreen led to confrontations with both her and her parents. He had been a wrestler in high school and his physical development during that period made him an intimidating figure to many people. At a meeting with both his and her parents, he denied breaking into the Jones' home and removing pictures of Noreen. After Gomer Jones later called the DiPiazza's, insisting that he felt Bennie had removed the missing pictures, Mr. DiPiazza discovered the pictures in his automobile and returned them. It was later learned that after Noreen had taken the bus from Little Falls and was upstairs in the Jones home, Bennie entered the first floor of the house and took the pictures. In 1963 Bennie stood outside of the Jones' home and yelled threats to the family. Gomer once again called the elder DiPiazza and pleaded with him to put an end to Bennie's harassment. When his father attempted to discipline him about the matter, Bennie struck his father and then left home for several days. It was during this time period that Noreen made the decision to leave the Ilion High School and transfer to Little Falls.

In March 1963 Bennie found Noreen's father Gomer at work in the Ilion High School gymnasium and approached him, yelling loudly, blaming him for not allowing his daughter to go out with him. He asked, "Why won't you let me see your daughter?" Mr. Jones answered, "I don't care who Noreen goes out with, but it is up to Noreen to decide who she dates." Bennie cursed him out and left as he had done on other occasions. That type of harassment eventually led to the decision by Noreen to transfer to St. Mary's Academy in Little Falls to complete her final year of high school; she moved into her Aunt Yolanda Speer's home near Little Falls. Noreen made the move because she felt threatened and would be alone in Ilion much of the time. Gomer was working multiple jobs, her mother Flora had gone to Erie, Pennsylvania to teach nursing and her brothers were away at college. Shortly after she had moved in with her aunt, an automobile pulled into the Speer's driveway one night about 3 a.m. and the driver shouted out, "Hey, hey, hey, I know you're in there." But when an outside light was turned on, the car drove away.

One of the strangest actions involving Bennie and the Jones home was his showing up one day on a bicycle, leaving the bicycle near the Jones' garage, getting a ride back to Frankfort and later showing up with a large tow truck to take the bike back home in Frankfort. No one understood that action and Noreen certainly couldn't have been impressed by his behavior.

In February 1964, Bennie came to the Jones family home on Main Street in Ilion and was able to seize an opportunity where he and Noreen were alone. The underlying purpose of his visit was to discuss a future where they would be together. He now suggested they get married after she graduated from college. When he was later asked about that meeting, Bennie recalled that she told him to get her off his mind, to forget about her entirely, and that she was going off to college. He said he was hurt and angry. When she later said he had hit her, he claimed he didn't remember doing that. It was the pivotal point leading to Noreen's parents asking for help from the Herkimer County District Attorney's Office to protect their daughter.

A meeting was set up to be held in the Ilion office of District Attorney Albert W. Schneider. All parties that were requested to be there showed up and included Noreen with her parents and Bennie with his parents. Ilion Police Judge James Curtis took charge. In an attempt to bring an end to the harassment, a demand was made in writing that Bennie promise not to have anything to do with Noreen Jones or any member of her family in the future. Schneider handed the document to Bennie and he signed his name to it. The Jones family felt relieved that the ongoing nightmare just might be over and when Schneider asked the parties to shake hands, they did.

The Jones family got up from their chairs and went to retrieve their coats. Suddenly, Bennie struck Noreen in the face with his fist. Her father, Gomer, came to the aid of his daughter who was sprawled out on the floor. Bennie now turned on him and the former high school wrestler picked him up and threw him onto a wooden bench that broke in half. That bench had a one inch board for a seat. Bennie jumped upon Gomer and began beating him violently before being pulled away by his own father.

The attack resulted in Bennie's arrest on assault charges and commitment to Utica State Hospital for a mental evaluation. Dr. George Volow, director of the hospital later certified that the young man was able "to comprehend the nature of the charges involving the altercation." A copy of the report was sent to both the DiPiazza family and the court. A hearing was held on March 13th. Acting Police Judge Samuel Lahey took charge of the proceedings after Police Judge James Curtis recused himself from the case.

Bennie was represented by Attorney George Aney and the defendant, no longer a teenager, was placed on two years probation after a judgment of two consecutive six–month sentences at Monroe County Penitentiary for third-degree assault was suspended by Judge Lahey. Any violation of his probation would subject him to a year of incarceration.

Four months into his probation, Bennie had trouble with his parents and after a heated argument with his father it was agreed that he would leave the Pleasant Avenue home and stay with his seventy-year-old grandfather in St. Louis, Missouri. Anthony DiPiazza had moved to St. Louis after his release from Auburn Prison where he had served his sentence for the second-degree Frankfort murder in 1932. He had been paroled, then set entirely free in 1961 and was offered a place to stay and a job in St. Louis after his release from Auburn. Now, his grandson was being given a similar offer to stay in St. Louis.

But Bennie returned to Frankfort in August 1964, after spending only a few weeks in St. Louis with his grandfather. He was cruising the streets of Frankfort in his father's car just before noon on August 27, 1964 and gave a ride to two sisters, one a junior and the other a senior at Frankfort High. When he dropped them off he continued on, stopping and speaking to others in the village including one of his cousins. Ten days earlier, an incident had occurred where he was once again standing near the Jones home, looking into the windows. This led to his driver's license being withdrawn. But he was driving, and during his journey, he discovered that Noreen and her father were in town. Gomer Jones' Cadillac was easy to spot that afternoon.

It was a happy day for Noreen. Earlier in the day she had gone on a shopping trip to Little Falls, selecting her college wardrobe. She had made many friends there, graduating from St. Mary's Academy, just a few months earlier. Her father had brought her to the Citizens First National Bank at the corner of Litchfield and Main streets in Frankfort, just a few blocks away from the DiPiazza home. Noreen was applying for a New York State higher education assistance loan after being accepted to Mary Regina College in Syracuse, a

Catholic junior college for women. She would be majoring in elementary education and during a phone conversation around 1 p.m. she told one of her best friends, Peggy Price of Ilion, that she was confident the loan would be approved and she could enter college in the following week.

While Noreen was inside the bank, Gomer waited on a bench that was in front of the bank, probably keeping an eye out for the highly visible pink Buick automobile that Bennie had been driving around the village. And sure enough, Bennie came along, driving the Buick. Gomer quickly left the bench and went inside the bank to escort his daughter out of the building. As they walked down the bank steps, there was Bennie, out of the car, standing on the sidewalk, watching them.

The Jones' car was not parked on Main Street and Gomer wanted to get his daughter away from DiPiazza as soon as possible. They hitched a ride with a van that was stopped at the intersection light and had the driver take them to the Irons residence only a few blocks away. There they met Noreen's aunt, Frances Irons, who was with Noreen back in 1961 when Noreen first met Bennie DiPiazza. Frances gave Gomer a ride to retrieve his car while Noreen tended to her young cousins. Before retrieving Gomer's Cadillac they stopped at the DiPiazza home, only a block away on Pleasant Avenue, intending to speak with Bennie's parents about their son's intimidating actions in front of the bank. They found that no one was home and drove away, soon encountering Bennie in the Buick. He threatened to ram their car if they didn't pull over and shouted "Gomer, you son of a bitch you. If you tell lies to my probation officer, I'm going to get you." Frances yelled back "Leave the Jones' alone, stay out of trouble." and they returned to the Irons' home.

Frances Irons called the Frankfort Police Department and Acting Police Chief George Grates answered the phone. The anxiety in Frances' voice was obvious and he responded immediately to the Irons' home, arriving about ten minutes before 2 p.m. Gomer told him that he was afraid of young DiPiazza, and expressed his opinion that Bennie was a dangerous person. The Buick was seen driving by the parked police car and quickly leaving the area so Grates left the residence to patrol the streets of the village in an attempt to find DiPiazza and warn him that he was violating the terms of his probation. Gomer meanwhile, attempted to contact Michael Bush, head of the Herkimer County Probation Department, but Mr. Bush was on vacation.

Noreen and her aunt felt more at ease after being told by Chief Grates that he would find DiPiazza and warn him about his actions. They decided to take the children to the Royal Market, only a block away, where they would buy ice cream for the children. But before they reached the market, Bennie pulled up to the curb and shouted to Noreen, "You, you're next." Noreen replied, "Bennie, what are you so steamed up about?" and Frances once again reminded him that if he stayed away, he would stay out of trouble.

Noreen, Frances and the two children changed plans quickly and instead of entering the Royal Market to buy ice cream, they headed for the Frankfort Police Station, a short distance around the corner. The actual police headquarters was located in the rear of the Village Hall building, a building usually occupied by a few village employees. On that afternoon, three people were in the village offices but the police headquarters was empty because George Grates was still out in his patrol car looking for Bennie DiPiazza. From the front door of the village hall, Noreen, Frances and the kids traveled down a long hallway to the police department. They passed Village Clerk Fred Petrell's office on the left. His barred door was usually locked, but was open that day. On the right they passed an area where the public came in to pay water and light bills. Mayme Salamone and Alice Spina were behind the payment windows that day.

Frances and the children went into Fred Petrell's office while Noreen sat in a chair in front of the police chief's desk. Francis asked Fred to call the Ilion Police Station and request they contact George Grates in the patrol car and have him return to his office. She explained that they were afraid that Bennie was following them. Mayme and Alice came across to Fred's office and joined the conversation. But they could never have imagined what all of them, including two small children, were about to witness. Noreen remained seated in the chair in the Police Department, terrified, but probably feeling protected from harm just by being in that location.

That location, at the end of the hallway had the best view to see anyone entering the building through the front door and Noreen's worst fear was realized. She jumped up and ran to the clerk's office where everyone was gathered, yelling that Bennie had entered the building and he had a gun in his hand. "He's got a gun" she screamed and in an instant a shot rang out. Upon a second shot, sixty-eight-year-old Fred Petrell, who had just hung up the phone after calling Ilion, put a bear hug on the intruder and attempted to deflect his aim, but more shots rang out and they had hit the target. Noreen had attempted to hide under the clerk's table but she lay on her back now in a pool of blood. Bennie had fired seven shots. It was over in seconds. He was only about three feet away from her when firing his eight chamber .380 caliber Beretta. She never had a chance.

Bennie looked at Fred and asked "Is she all right?" Fred later told a reporter that "he looked like he was hunting, shooting at an animal. Then he had the nerve to ask me if she was alright." An autopsy report would later show that death was from "hemorrhage of the chest and abdomen due to multiple bullet wounds." It was Fred, almost five decades older than Bennie, that knocked the gun out of the killer's hand by punching his elbow. The two of them wrestled into the police department and lock-up area of the building. DiPiazza wanted to run but Fred held him in his grasp. "Freddy, let me go, let me go, I've got to get the hell out of here" was heard by the witnesses. Aunt Frances Irons struck Bennie with a food blender she had been carrying and then Chief Grates arrived. Fred yelled out "Pull your gun, George, he's just killed that poor little girl." Chief Grates incarcerated Bennie to await the arrival of the state police. At a trial a year later, Grates testified that Bennie told him, "They made me do it. I had to do it."

It was only six months earlier that Herkimer County police units had responded to the Lucie Dade murder only several hundred feet away. Once again the village was in shock as word spread throughout the Mohawk Valley. Another of Noreen's aunts from the large Frankfort family, had arrived at the village hall shortly after the shooting. Miss Mary Stabile lived just around the corner from the scene of the shooting and was following her sister and niece into the building, heard shots ring out and ran screaming back out to Main Street where a crowd started gathering, eventually growing to three hundred onlookers.

Ambulance service at that time had to come from Herkimer or Ilion and emergency crews from both villages responded. But when they arrived, Dr. Ernest Enzien had already pronounced Noreen dead. Dr. Ladislaus Merson went to Rose and Margaret Trois' dress shop, directly across from the village hall. There he tended to Gomer and other relatives and close friends that were distraught, and later to Noreen's mother, Flora. The Reverend Michael Fufferd and the Reverend Gregory Mulhall, priests from Frankfort and Ilion shuttled between the dress shop and village offices through the growing crowd to console those in both places. Noreen's brother Brian had been driven to Frankfort from his job at Remington Arms and his uncle, Trooper Allen Irons, went to Utica to find Flora at work and console her professionally about the terrible news, but she had left on her normal route to Ilion which took her directly into the West Main Street crowd. As Brian was crossing the crowded street he spotted his mom's car, opened the passenger-side door and when Flora asked what was going on, he had to tell her what no mother should ever have to hear.

The shooters father, now village police judge, was located in Syracuse and when informed of what had taken place uttered one short reply, "Oh my God, no." Asked about the gun, Mr. DiPiazza said he had no idea his son had a gun and didn't know where he even would have gotten a gun.

Later in the day, rumors started circulating about revenge and threats to the shooter and officials involved in the shooter's probation. Gomer Jones had told many people that after Bennie had cruised by and also looked into the windows of the Jones' home on the previous Monday evening, he had called the head of the Herkimer County Probation Department, Michael Bush, at 11 p.m. to report this obvious violation of Bennie's probation. Gomer said Bush "Gave me hell for calling him at home." On Tuesday morning Gomer had called Herkimer County Judge Edmund McCarthy to complain about DiPiazza's actions and Bush's lack of action as Bennie's probation officer. Several members of the Jones family made statements to the press indicating their feelings that there was an atmosphere of protection around the son of a police judge in Frankfort by politicians, school officials and even some in law enforcement.

There was tension in the air when it was time to transport Bennie to the Herkimer County Jail. Acting Police Chief George Grates called in four of his part-time officers after he had heard about threats to DiPiazza from both Ilion and Frankfort. A force of several state troopers arrived to perform the transfer. Michael Bush told police that he had received several threatening phone calls and he and his family actually left their home to go into hiding.

Bennie was heavily guarded on the Friday following the previous day's shooting. His arraignment was scheduled to be in front of Peace Justice George Murtaugh in the Frankfort Town Hall. Only about two dozen people were outside waiting when the prisoner was brought back to Frankfort. His father was in attendance when Attorney George Aney asked for an adjournment until Monday, saying he was seeking additional counsel for his client. District Attorney Albert Schneider did not object and the adjournment was granted by Judge Murtaugh. The 10 a.m. Monday arraignment plan was widely publicized and on Monday a crowd estimated at four hundred people lined Litchfield Street across from the town hall to catch a glimpse of and shout epithets at Bennie as he was escorted into the building surrounded by a heavy guard of officers.

Arraignment took place only minutes after the funeral procession had proceeded along Main Street to Mount Olivet Cemetery. The Church of the Annunciation in Ilion was filled to capacity for Noreen's solemn requiem mass. It was estimated that over fifteen hundred people paid their respects at the funeral home and church. As the funeral was about to start, a steady summer downpour began. Bearers were classmates of Noreen at St. Mary's Academy, six boys. Six other boys and ten female classmates provided an honor escort.

The arraignment was closed to the public after District Attorney Albert Schneider objected to the presence of news reporters. "I don't want to give the case any more publicity than it already has had," the D.A. said. "I don't want to be accused of trying the case in the newspapers."

Within forty-eight hours after the shooting, the gun used in the tragedy was identified as a stolen weapon. The eight shot, .380 Beretta automatic handgun was reported stolen from the locked glove box in an automobile parked in downtown Utica. It had been reported stolen by its licensed owner nearly a year earlier on September 28, 1963. State

Police Investigator William G. Glasser questioned Bennie about his possession of the stolen weapon and received conflicting responses. First he claimed a friend had given the gun to him but later said he found it in a dump. The weapon had no rust on it and an unsuccessful attempt had been made to remove the serial number. When Glasser questioned Bennie about the ammunition used, he also received an ambiguous reply. Bennie said he bought bullets in a store, but didn't remember where. When the gun was stolen, eight or nine bullets were also reported taken with it. A later report claimed DiPiazza may have purchased ammunition during his two week stay in St. Louis.

By October, the case went to the grand jury and on October 21,1964 Benedict X. DiPiazza was indicted for first degree murder, a charge that could result in the death penalty. His attorney, Henry E. Taylor of Syracuse, entered a plea of innocent by reason of insanity and asked the court for a mental examination of the twenty year old. A hearing to discuss the request was held on October 29th. At that meeting, District Attorney Albert W. Schneider made a motion to dismiss Attorney Taylor's request because DiPiazza had already been in a mental hospital in February and at that time had been ruled fully competent to understand the assault charges against him.

The defense was later allowed to have DiPiazza taken to the Syracuse office of Dr. Sidney A. Orgel, a psychologist and to have Dr. Eugene N. Boudreau, also of Syracuse, interview DiPiazza in the Herkimer County Jail and his parents at their home. Early in 1965, Attorney Henry E. Taylor argued before the Rochester Court Appellate Division that his client could not get a fair trial in Herkimer County, claiming there had been undue publicity and, as a result, mass prejudice developed. The request for a change of venue was denied and an April trial was scheduled in the Herkimer County Courthouse. Because of his previous involvement in Bennie DiPiazza's probation case, Herkimer County Judge Edmund A. McCarthy requested that a judge from another county be assigned to the trial. Judge George R. Davis from Lewis County was selected.

Jury selection was a long and tedious process. Judge Davis presided during a two week period, calling over two hundred and fifty county residents in an attempt to seat twelve jurors. By April 28th, a jury of eight men and four women was seated and the first degree murder trial began. The number of witnesses that were inside the village hall and saw the tragic shooting left no doubt as to what happened that day. The defense's claim that DiPiazza was insane when he committed the crime was the key issue to be decided.

Psychologist Dr. Sidney A. Orgel testified as an expert witness for the defense. He described DiPiazza as a person who could go into a rage with little provocation. Dr. Orgel described a series of tests conducted at his office in Syracuse. Verbal and performance tests for the Wrexler-Bellevue Scale used for estimating intellectual brightness indicated that DiPiazza's IQ was 122 in verbal, 117 in performance and 122 at full-scale. This put DiPiazza in a superior range, equal to or better than about 95 of 100 persons in the same age group. In the Rorschach (ink blot) test, DiPiazza answered questions in 4 to 6 seconds that normally take 10 to 20 seconds for responses. Dr. Orgel claimed that this indicated little capacity to delay impulsive reactions, "an act first, think later" personality. He said DiPiazza showed feelings of inadequacy, tense hostility, destruction and sadism. He described DiPiazza as having to prove to himself and to others that he was a male as competent as any other male, chronically antisocial, maintains no loyalty, is frequently callous and shows a gross lack of responsibility and exercise of judgment. When asked about his diagnosis of DiPiazza's behavior, Dr. Orgel said DiPiazza could be termed a psychopathic individual or, in modern terms, a sociopath. He claimed that the shooting of all the bullets in the gun at one time appeared to him to be "the symbolic discharge of all that had been built up in him" and added that in his opinion, DiPiazza would not have a memory of the events of the shooting, that amnesia was frequently seen in cases like this.

Dr. Eugene N. Boudreau, a psychiatrist, was then called as a witness for the defense. His conclusion, gained after he had interviewed both the defendant and his parents, backed the testimony of Dr. Orgel. They both described DiPiazza as having a psychopathic personality, emotionally unstable, and with psychosis, was not capable of differentiating between right and wrong and did not know the nature or quality of the act he was being tried for. A surprise rebuttal witness to Dr. Orgel's testimony was Sheriff Richard W. Folts who had taken DiPiazza to Syracuse for Dr. Orgel's testing. He claimed that before he returned to Herkimer with the defendant, Dr. Orgel had told him "If I were to come down as a witness for the defense, it would do no good. He (DiPiazza) is normal, but has a hot temper." Defense Attorney Henry Taylor asked Folts if he was in court when Dr. Orgel said he recalled no such conversation. Folts answered in the negative.

The district attorney put Dr. Irving Jacobs on the stand to counter the insanity claim of the Syracuse doctors. He had interviewed DiPiazza at Marcy State Hospital during a five-week stay there. His test results showed a psychopathic personality without psychosis or "legal insanity." To even the playing field, the district attorney called Dr. Newton Bigelow, Marcy State Hospital administrator, as his last witness on the twenty-seventh day of the trial. Dr. Bigelow backed testimony given by Dr. Jacobs by stating that they both contended that DiPiazza, on the murder date, was: capable of differentiating between right and wrong, knew and understood the nature and quality of his acts, and that he was capable of premeditating an act, deliberating the act, and of forming conscious intent or design to effect the death of Noreen Jones.

The trial lasted thirty days. On Friday, May 21, 1965, the jurors, eight men and four women, received the case. After twenty-three hours (that included over sixteen hours of deliberation and a six hour stay in a motel at 3:30 a.m. to get some sleep) they convicted Benedict X. DiPiazza of first-degree murder. His parents and those of Noreen Jones sat in the front row of the Herkimer County courtroom where one hundred others sat as another one hundred onlookers waited outside the courthouse. The clock on the steeple of historic Dutch Reformed Church finished tolling twelve noon as the last juror announced his verdict. DiPiazza became the first person in forty-four years to be convicted of first-degree murder in Herkimer County. The last was Rutger B. Warder, sentenced to die in the electric chair, but later paroled (as described in Chapter 8). On the Tuesday following the jury's determination of DiPiazza's guilt, Judge George R. Davis was obligated to follow new legislation, passed a year earlier, giving guidance regarding sentencing rules.

The law gave the judge these options:

He could discharge the jury and impose a life sentence if satisfied the death was unwarranted by substantial or mitigating circumstances.

He could ask the jury to decide the life or death penalty. Both the prosecutor and defense could submit evidence concerning relevant matters regarding the nature and circumstances of the crime.

If the jury failed to agree, the judge could impanel a new jury for sentence, or impose a life term.

But Judge Davis said he believed it was his responsibility and pronounced a sentence of life in prison with a minimum of twenty years. Death penalty laws were in the process of re-examination at the time and the last execution by electric chair took place in 1963. Shortly after DiPiazza's conviction, legislation was enacted limiting the death penalty only to murder in the first degree when the victim was a peace officer. After sentencing, Bennie was taken to Elmira Reception Center to be classified for imprisonment.

After he was sent to prison, DiPiazza, using another Syracuse attorney named John E. Shaffer began an appeal for a reversal and a new trial. Shaffer declared in the state's highest court that his client "could not get a fair trial in

Herkimer County." He cited pretrial publicity appearing in the Utica Observer Dispatch, The Utica Daily Press and the Herkimer Telegram newspapers. He also asked for a reversal on the ground that his client was insane at the time of the crime. But in writing the court's opinion, Chief Judge Stanley Fuld of the Court of Appeals said "Although the community was small and the defendant's crime was widely known, the pretrial newspaper accounts were surprisingly objective." "In short," he said, "the record demonstrates that the publicity was not of such a character as to require a change of venue." As to DiPiazza being insane at the time of the crime, Judge Fuld said the jury had plenty of testimony by professionals to make a proper judgment on that issue. On April 10, 1969 the Court of Appeals unanimously upheld DiPiazza's first degree murder conviction. In the two years following that ruling, appeals to re-argue the case were denied by Federal District Court judges.

After twenty years of incarceration, Bennie applied for parole, seeking to return to Frankfort. A 1984 request to return home at Christmas time was denied after Herkimer County District Attorney Henry LaRaia strongly opposed it. In 1989 he underwent another psychiatric evaluation and beyond that time period he realized that continuing threats he had been making to various family members and police were not helping him achieve parole status. In the following years, succeeding D.A.'s continued to fight any attempt by Bennie to return to Herkimer County. The family of Noreen Jones was always represented at the parole hearings and made the board aware that they felt threatened by his possible release. By 1996 DiPiazza had been denied parole six times.

A February 1996 parole hearing was noted by the conspicuous absence of anyone from Noreen's family and the Herkimer County District Attorney, Michael E. Daley. The lack of objection to DiPiazza's release led to the board voting that Bennie could be released if a proper location could be found for him to live. When the Jones family discovered what had happened in February, they, along with D.A. Michael Daley demanded a re-investigation into what had occurred, claiming neither the D.A. or the family were notified in advance that a hearing would take place.

By June, the parole board, which now had been subject to strong protests from the public, ruled that DiPiazza could not return to Frankfort to live when released. For two years, DiPiazza sat in his cell as the protest continued against his returning to the Mohawk Valley. But at the same time, a group of his friends and relatives worked to get him released and settled back in Frankfort. That group was successful in getting the Frankfort Town Board involved in the matter. During the period from July through August 1998, three letters, each written by two village trustees, the mayor and the town supervisor had been sent to the state parole board, all stating that they had no knowledge of any protest documents opposing the release of DiPiazza to Frankfort.

On December 29, 1998, Herkimer County D.A. Michael E. Daley led a group of protesters who attended a town board meeting to criticize the content of the letters sent to the parole board by town and village officials. During the time of protest by the Jones family and friends, DiPiazza's lawyers had used those letters with their motion to release as evidence that their client could return to Frankfort. It was stated in those motion papers that a job was waiting for DiPiazza at Montana's Sports Bar at North Litchfield Street in Frankfort and that DiPiazza had a place to live with his father on Pleasant Avenue in Frankfort. At the January 5, 1999 Frankfort Town Board meeting, seventeen friends and relatives of DiPiazza spoke in support of DiPiazza's return to Frankfort. The town board agreed to fax a letter to the senior parole officer before a scheduled January 9th hearing, stating that the board was neutral on the topic of DiPiazza's return to Frankfort.

Protests from the Jones' side continued and D.A. Daley attended the January 11th hearing, presenting arguments against DiPiazza's return. A busload of Mohawk Valley residents accompanied Daley, including Noreen's mother, Aunt Frances Irons, and brothers Brian and George. The courtroom was packed, a very unusual event for that type of hearing. The assistant to the state attorney general argued that the division of parole had made many attempts to find Bennie a home. California, Vermont, the City of Utica and three hotels in Syracuse were mentioned. It was stated that these efforts were found unacceptable by the division of parole or not possible because his own family members refused to allow him to live with them. It was ruled that Bennie DiPiazza cannot move back to Frankfort or anywhere near Frankfort.

In spite of the protests, on August 30, 1999, Benedict Xavier DiPiazza, who now had been incarcerated in the New York criminal justice system for thirty-five years, was released from prison but required to live in the Albany area and not to return to Frankfort, New York. But that lasted only fifteen weeks because on December 14, 1999 he was found to be in possession of a weapon, a bow and arrow and was arrested for shoplifting about two hundred fifty dollars worth of merchandise at Albany Crossgates Mall. He was immediately returned to prison. In the twenty-first century there have been parole denials issued every few years. In 2008, State Senator James Seward wrote a letter to the parole board saying he objected to any consideration of parole "in the strongest possible terms" out of concern for the family and his constituents. In 2010 parole was denied and in 2012 the board told him he was unfit for release and that they felt the risk of him breaking the law again was too great to release him. In 2014, fifty years after the shooting, Benedict X. DiPiazza was again told by the parole board that he would continue to serve his life sentence.

Fifty years should not diminish the memory of what was taken away from the Jones family and the communities of Frankfort and Ilion that hot August afternoon in 1964 by the actions of one person. Noreen had unlimited potential to impact the lives of students in a classroom somewhere. On the following page is a copy of an article printed in The Ilion Sentinel newspaper in 1954 when she was only eight.

TROOP 26

by Noreen Jones

Our last three meetings have been spent in making Christmas gifts for our parents, and I cannot tell you what we have made until after Christmas, since it is a secret operation.

At our meeting of Nov. 2, we learned the Brownie Scout Promise and we discussed the meaning of it and how it differs from the Girl Scout Promise. We also talked about the Girl Scout Laws. At our next meeting we opened with a Pledge of Allegiance and continued working on our projects, under the direction of our leaders; Mrs. George Jones and Mrs. James Staring, we closed with The Brownie Scout Promise. At the Nov. 22 meeting we opened with the Promise followed with refreshments; we serve refreshments at each meeting with the girls taking turns at being hostess; after we played a few games. We also have learned the meaning of the brownies, a story was read to us at the Nov. 29th meeting about them.

We have decided to hold Investure services on Dec. 13 and we also decided to invite our mothers. At that time we will become full-fledged Brownies.

About the Author

Bill Schuster spent his first forty years in Frankfort before moving to a hobby farm in the Town of New Hartford. He worked at Union Tools in Frankfort. At Union he retired before the plant closed and had been its plant and chief engineer. A holder of three patents, he owned his own company supplying products to the equine industry. The business developed out of his involvement in racing harness horses for two decades. His first book, Stories Forgotten Frankfort, N.Y. was a retirement project. It is basically the only modern day history of the village. In researching village history he found the stories included in this book. He was able to interview family members descended from those involved in the cases presented. Some of them said they had never been told many of the details presented in this work.

Acknowledgments

Once again, the author gratefully thanks Tom Tryniski for his amazing website fultonhistory.com where he has placed millions of digitized newspaper pages online for public use at his expense. Everyone interested in the stories compiled in this book should visit the search engine on the website and also visit Frankfort's wonderful library and observe what has been preserved of the village's past.

Made in the USA
Las Vegas, NV
20 February 2021